CW00557049

ISBN 978-0-265-07770-2
PIBN 10948966

he Commercial Club of Chicago

THE COMMERCIAL CLUB, ORGANIZED 1877
THE MERCHANTS CLUB, ORGANIZED 1896
UNITED 1907

Year-Book
1922-23

PUBLISHED BY
THE EXECUTIVE COMMITTEE
1923

The Lakeside Press
R. R. DONNELLEY & SONS COMPANY
CHICAGO

TABLE OF CONTENTS

THE COMMERCIAL CLUB OF CHICAGO

ARTICLES OF ASSOCIATION

THE COMMERCIAL CLUB, organized December 27, 1877, and THE MERCHANTS CLUB OF CHICAGO, organized December 11, 1896, more efficiently to advance the public welfare and the commercial interests of Chicago by co-operative effort, social intercourse, and a free interchange of views, were united February 11, 1907, under the name of THE COMMERCIAL CLUB OF CHICAGO.

Its Articles of Association are as follows:

ARTICLE I.

MEMBERS.

1. The membership shall be of four classes: Active, Associate, Non-resident and Retired.

2. Active Members are responsible for the varied undertakings of the Club, and will accept and perform, within reasonable limitations, the assignment of work by the Executive Committee to advance the Club's interests. They shall be not more than fifty-five years old at the time of their election, and their number shall not exceed one hundred twenty-five men.

3. An Associate Member shall have the same rights and duties as an Active Member, except that he shall not be obliged to serve as an officer or required to do active work for the Club save under special circumstances, and that he shall not be fined for absence from Club meetings. Any Active Member, upon reaching the age of sixty-five years,

may, at his written request to the Executive Committee, become an Associate Member.

4. Any Active or Associate Member who has permanently removed from Chicago may, upon application to the Executive Committee, and with its approval, become a Non-resident Member.

5. Non-resident and Retired Members shall have the privilege of attending all meetings of the Club, but shall not be entitled to vote.

6. The present Retired Membership shall not be increased except by transfer, upon their request, of Charter Members of the Commercial Club.

7. The Secretary shall notify the members whenever a vacancy in the Active Membership occurs.

It is the duty of members to submit to the Secretary for the information of the Executive Committee names of citizens eligible for membership by reason of their personality, general reputation, and their contributions in effective interest and service to the common welfare. Each nominee must receive the unanimous vote of the Executive Committee, and thereupon the Secretary will notify the members that the nominee will be voted upon at the next meeting of the Club. Any member who has objection to the nominee must immediately advise a member of the Executive Committee thereof. Two weeks must elapse between the date of notice and the meeting at which the vote is taken. The voting shall be by ballot, and three negative votes shall defer the admission of such nominee. If the names of two or more nominees are printed on the ballot, opportunity will be given to cast a separate vote for each nominee.

8. In the approval of candidates regard shall be had, so far as practicable, to the branches of business, or professions, in which they are engaged, so that the various interests of the city shall be fairly represented in the membership.

9. The Executive Committee is authorized to elect by unanimous vote, during any Club year, one person ineligible to Active Membership because of age, to Associate Membership, in recognition of distinguished service rendered by him.

10. Each Active and Associate Member shall pay, November 1st, annual dues of seventy-five dollars, which shall cover the cost of dinners at regular meetings. Non-resident and Retired Members shall not be required to pay dues, but only an assessment for each dinner which they attend or which they notify the Secretary that they will attend.

The Executive Committee may drop from the roll any member who, after due notification of dues, fails to pay them within thirty days.

ARTICLE II.

OFFICERS AND COMMITTEES.

1. The Officers shall be a President, a Vice-President, a Secretary and a Treasurer. An Executive Committee of twelve members shall have general control of the affairs of the Club. It shall consist of the four officers, the Secretary of the preceding year, if a new Secretary is elected, the Chairman of the Reception Committee, and six other members, or seven other members if the Secretary of the preceding year is re-elected.

2. At the April meeting the officers and Reception Committee shall be elected to serve for one year, and two of the four elective members of the Executive Committee shall be elected to serve for two years, and until their respective successors are elected and qualify. The Club year shall be from installation of officers, at the annual meeting, to the installation of their successors. If the Secretary of the

preceding year is re-elected, a fifth elective member of the Executive Committee shall be elected to serve for one year.

3. The President—or, in his absence, the Vice-President—shall preside at all meetings of the Club and of the Executive Committee.

4. The Secretary shall make and preserve complete records of all meetings of the Club and of the Executive Committee, keep all its books and papers, and perform such other duties as may be required by the Club, or by the Executive Committee. He shall also prepare the Year-Book, in which shall be printed the list of officers, committees, and meetings since April, 1907. In all Club publications the names of The Commercial Club and The Merchants Club should appear, with the dates of their organizations and the date of their union.

5. The Treasurer shall receive and keep the funds of the Club, and shall disburse the same, subject to the supervision of the Executive Committee, and shall keep an accurate record thereof. He shall make a full financial report at the annual April meeting. His books shall be open at all times to the inspection of the Executive Committee and of an Examiner, whom the Executive Committee should appoint before the April meeting, to audit the same.

6. The Executive Committee shall have power, by unanimous vote of the entire Committee, to discipline or expel any Club member whenever in its judgment such action is advisable.

7. A Reception Committee, consisting of a Chairman (who shall be *ex officio* a member of the Executive Committee) and four members, shall be elected annually at the April meeting. Its duties shall be to assist in the entertainment of the Club's guests and its new members, and to act in a general way as the hosts of the Club, subject to the direction of the Executive Committee.

8. The President, with the advice and approval of the Executive Committee, shall select a Nominating Committee of five members and announce their names at the regular March meeting. Such committee shall recommend a list of candidates for the various offices and elective committees, and file the same with the Secretary at least twenty days before the April meeting. The Secretary shall mail such list to each member at least two weeks before the April meeting for the annual election.

ARTICLE III.

MEETINGS.

1. The Club shall hold meetings on the second Friday in October, November, December, January, April, and May.

The Executive Committee shall select the place for each meeting, and may, in its discretion, change the date of any meeting or omit any meeting, or call special meetings at any time.

2. The Secretary shall mail to each member notice of each meeting at least five days before its date. The notice shall state specifically if any nominee for membership is to be voted upon at such meeting and any other business that is to be transacted. At any regular or special meeting, at which thirty Active Members are present, any business of the Club may be transacted.

3. The regular meetings of the Club shall take precedence of all social engagements. Written notice of inability to attend a regular meeting, with the reason therefor, shall be sent to the Secretary so as to reach him by the morning of the day of such regular meeting. Any member failing to give such notice, or whose reason for non-attendance is unsatisfactory to the Executive Committee, shall be fined ten dollars. Repeated instances of

non-attendance, not satisfactorily explained, shall be construed as a lack of interest in the Club and its activities and, in such cases, the Executive Committee is empowered and directed to cancel the membership.

ARTICLE IV.

GUESTS.

With the permission of the Executive Committee, expressed in the notice of the meeting, any member may invite the number of guests specified in the notice; but no person shall be a guest of the same member at more than two dinners during the Club year.

ARTICLE V.

AMENDMENTS.

These Articles may be altered or amended at any meeting by a majority vote of the Active and Associate Members present, provided that notice of each proposed amendment was given at a prior meeting and was stated in the notice of the meeting at which the amendment is to be voted upon.

Officers and Committees
of
The Commercial Club of Chicago

THE COMMERCIAL CLUB, ORGANIZED 1877
THE MERCHANTS CLUB, ORGANIZED 1896
UNITED 1907

OFFICERS AND COMMITTEES OF THE COMMERCIAL CLUB OF CHICAGO

1923–1924

President . . . . Harry A. Wheeler
Vice-President . . . . Frederic W. Upham
Secretary . . . . George E. Scott
Treasurer . . . . Albert W. Harris

EXECUTIVE COMMITTEE

Joseph M. Cudahy
Samuel M. Felton
Albert W. Harris
Clarence S. Pellet
George E. Scott
Robert W. Stewart
Frederic W. Upham
Harry A. Wheeler
Thomas E. Wilson
Wallace C. Winter

RECEPTION COMMITTEE

Wallace C. Winter, Chairman
William P. Sidley
Leonard A. Busby
John Stuart
Robert J. Thorne

COMMITTEE ON COMMUNITY CHEST

Walter H. Wilson, Chairman
Edward F. Carry
Edward L. Ryerson
George E. Scott
John W. Scott
Julius Rosenwald
T. W. Robinson

COMMITTEE ON EDUCATIONAL INSTITUTIONS

Rufus C. Dawes, Chairman

Joy Morton
William P. Sidley
Solomon A. Smith
Ezra J. Warner
Oliver T. Wilson
John T. McCutcheon
Theodore Robinson
John V. Farwell

COMMITTEE ON PLAN ON REVISION OF THE CONSTITUTION AND LEGISLATION

Silas H. Strawn, Chairman

Edgar A. Bancroft
Joseph E. Otis
Sewell L. Avery
Alexander H. Revell
Harrison B. Riley
B. A. Eckhart
Walter H. Wilson

COMMITTEE ON PLAN OF CHICAGO

Leonard A. Busby, Chairman
Alex Legge, Vice-Chairman

Eugene J. Buffington
W. Rufus Abbott
Frank S. Cunningham
Charles H. Markham
Donald R. McLennan
Harrison B. Riley
Charles H. Thorne
F. O. Wetmore

COMMITTEE ON WATER TRANSPORTATION

James O. Heyworth, Chairman
James Simpson, Vice-Chairman

Frederick H. Rawson
Edward F. Carry
Robert P. Lamont
Cyrus H. McCormick
Charles Piez
Charles H. Schweppe
Benjamin Carpenter
Hale Holden

1922–1923

President	Bernard E. Sunny
Vice-President	Donald R. McLennan
Secretary	Joseph M. Cudahy
Treasurer	Joseph E. Otis

EXECUTIVE COMMITTEE

Bernard E. Sunny
Donald R. McLennan
Joseph M. Cudahy
Joseph E. Otis

Sewell L. Avery
Samuel M. Felton
Victor F. Lawson
George E. Scott
John W. Scott
Thomas E. Wilson

RECEPTION COMMITTEE

George E. Scott, Chairman

Eugene J. Buffington
Benjamin Carpenter
Albert W. Harris
James Simpson

COMMITTEE ON PLAN OF CHICAGO

Leonard A. Busby, Chairman
Alex Legge, Vice-Chairman

Eugene J. Buffington
Rufus C. Dawes
Louis A. Ferguson
C. H. Markham
Clarence S. Pellet
Harrison B. Riley
Charles L. Strobel
Charles H. Thorne
Frank O. Wetmore

COMMITTEE ON AMERICAN MERCHANT MARINE

James O. Heyworth, Chairman
Frederic W. Upham, Vice-Chairman

H. M. Byllesby
Edward F. Carry
Robert P. Lamont
Cyrus H. McCormick
Charles Piez
James Simpson
Robert W. Stewart
H. A. Wheeler

COMMITTEE ON COMMUNITY CHEST

Walter H. Wilson, Chairman

Edward F. Carry
E. D. Hulbert
George E. Scott
John W. Scott
Julius Rosenwald
T. W. Robinson

COMMITTEE ON FORT SHERIDAN AND GREAT LAKES NAVAL TRAINING STATION

John T. Pirie, Chairman

Charles G. Dawes
H. M. Byllesby
Ezra J. Warner
E. D. Hulbert
E. N. Hurley
A. A. Sprague

COMMITTEE ON PLAN ON REVISION OF THE CONSTITUTION AND LEGISLATION

Silas H. Strawn, Chairman

Edgar A. Bancroft
Rufus C. Dawes
Hale Holden
Alexander H. Revell
Harrison B. Riley
Frederic W. Upham
Walter H. Wilson

COMMITTEE ON EDUCATIONAL INSTITUTIONS

Rufus C. Dawes, Chairman

Joy Morton
Martin A. Ryerson
William P. Sidley
Solomon A. Smith
Ezra J. Warner
Oliver T. Wilson

ACTIVE MEMBERS

1923 W. Rufus Abbott
President Illinois Bell Telephone Co.

1917 Sewell L. Avery
President United States Gypsum Co.

1899 Alfred L. Baker
Alfred L. Baker & Co.

1898 Edgar A. Bancroft
Scott, Bancroft, Martin & MacLeish

1902 Eugene J. Buffington
President Illinois Steel Co.

1918 Leonard A. Busby
President Chicago City Railway Co.

1913 H. M. Byllesby
President H. M. Byllesby & Co.

1914 Augustus A. Carpenter
Vice-President Ayer & Lord Tie Co.

1896 Benjamin Carpenter
President Geo. B. Carpenter & Co

1904 Edward F. Carry
President Pullman Company

1901 William E. Clow
President James B. Clow & Sons

1898 Alfred Cowles
332 South La Salle Street

1915 Richard T. Crane, Jr.
President Crane Company

1914 Joseph M. Cudahy
Vice-President Sinclair Consolidated Oil Corporation

1921 Frank S. Cunningham
President Butler Brothers

1922 Brig. Gen. Abel Davis
Vice-President Chicago Title & Trust Co.

1902 Charles G. Dawes
Chairman Board of Directors Central Trust Company of Illinois

1915 Rufus C. Dawes
Public Utilities

1911 Albert B. Dick
President A. B. Dick Co.

1902 Thomas E. Donnelley
President R. R. Donnelley & Sons Co.

1898 Bernard A. Eckhart
President B. A. Eckhart Milling Co.

1913 Howard Elting
President Heath & Milligan Mfg. Co.

1902 Francis C. Farwell
Treasurer John V. Farwell Co.

1896 John V. Farwell
President John V. Farwell Co.

1906 Samuel M. Felton
President Chicago Great Western R. R. Co.

1902 David R. Forgan
President National City Bank of Chicago

1884 John J. Glessner
Vice-President International Harvester Co.

1897 Ernest A. Hamill
Chairman Board of Directors Corn Exchange National Bank

1916 Albert W. Harris
Chairman Board of Directors Harris Trust & Savings Bank

1914 James O. Heyworth
M. Am. Soc. C. E., General Contractor

1915 Hale Holden
President Chicago, Burlington & Quincy R. R. Co.

1917 Edward N. Hurley
Manufacturer

1882 Charles L. Hutchinson
Vice-President Corn Exchange National Bank

1915 Robert P. Lamont
President American Steel Foundries

1899 Victor F. Lawson
President The Chicago Daily News Co.

1919 Alex. Legge
President International Harvester Co.

1885 Cyrus H. McCormick
Chairman Board of Directors International Harvester Co.

1898 Harold F. McCormick
International Harvester Co.

1904 Medill McCormick
1116 Century Building

1922 John T. McCutcheon
Chicago Tribune

1916 Donald R. McLennan
Marsh & McLennan

1901 Clayton Mark
Director National Malleable Castings Co.

1912 Charles H. Markham
President Illinois Central Railroad Company

1896 Arthur Meeker
Vice-President Armour & Co.

1901 George Merryweather
Highland Park, Ill.

1901 Joy Morton
Joy Morton & Co.

1906 Mark Morton
President Western Cold Storage Co.

1904 Joseph E. Otis
President Central Trust Company of Illinois

1914 Clarence S. Pellet
Fire Insurance

1917 Charles Piez
President and Treasurer Link Belt Company

1914 John T. Pirie
Carson, Pirie, Scott & Co.

1913 H. H. Porter
1005 First National Bank Building

1922 Frederick H. Rawson
President Union Trust Co.

1896 Alexander H. Revell
President Alexander H. Revell & Co.

1910 George M. Reynolds
Chairman Board of Directors The Continental and Commercial National Bank of Chicago

1912 Harrison B. Riley
President Chicago Title and Trust Co.

1903 Theodore W. Robinson
First Vice-President Illinois Steel Co.

1910 Julius Rosenwald
President Sears, Roebuck & Co.

1922 Edward L. Ryerson, Jr.
Vice-President Joseph T. Ryerson & Son

1922 Charles H. Schweppe
Lee Higginson & Co.

1920 George E. Scott
Vice-President American Steel Foundries

1905 John W. Scott
Carson, Pirie, Scott & Co.

1896 Louis A. Seeberger
Louis A. Seeberger & Co.

1897 John G. Shedd
Chairman Board of Directors Marshall Field & Co.

1922 William P. Sidley
Cutting, Moore & Sidley

1915 James Simpson
President Marshall Field & Co.

1915 Solomon A. Smith
President The Northern Trust Company

1904 Walter B. Smith
50 South La Salle Street

1903 Albert A. Sprague
Sprague, Warner & Co.

1919 Robert W. Stewart
Chairman Board of Directors Standard Oil Company of Indiana

1920 Silas H. Strawn
38 South Dearborn Street

1919 John Stuart
President Quaker Oats Co.

1906 Edward F. Swift
Vice-President Swift & Co.

1902 Charles H. Thorne

1917 Robert J. Thorne

1899 Frederic W. Upham
President Consumers Company

1897 Charles H. Wacker
Real Estate

1915 Ezra J. Warner
President Sprague, Warner & Co.

1916 Frank O. Wetmore
President First National Bank of Chicago

1912 Harry A. Wheeler
Vice-President Union Trust Co.

1905 John E. Wilder
President Wilder & Co.

1916 Oliver T. Wilson
Wilson Brothers

1919 Thomas E. Wilson
President Wilson & Co.

1896 Walter H. Wilson
Walter H. Wilson & Co.

1918 Wallace C. Winter
Broker—Farnum, Winter & Co.

ASSOCIATE MEMBERS

1899 Arthur T. Aldis
Real Estate

1901 J. Ogden Armour
President Armour & Co.

1889 Edward E. Ayer
Chairman Board of Directors Ayer & Lord Tie Co.

1901 William L. Brown
President Pickands, Brown & Co.

1896 Edward B. Butler
Chairman Board of Directors Butler Brothers

1906 Clyde M. Carr
President Joseph T. Ryerson & Son

1894 William J. Chalmers
Manufacturer

1904 J. J. Dau
Chairman Board of Directors Reid, Murdoch & Co.

1897 Albert J. Earling

1899 Louis A. Ferguson
Vice-President Commonwealth Edison Co.

1902 James B. Forgan
Chairman Board of Directors First National Bank of Chicago

1878 Marvin Hughitt
Chairman Board of Directors Chicago & North Western Railway Co.

1900 Charles H. Hulburd
President Elgin National Watch Co.

1899 Samuel Insull
President Commonwealth Edison Co.

1898 David B. Jones
President Mineral Point Zinc Co.

1900 Chauncey Keep

1896 Rollin A. Keyes
President Franklin MacVeagh & Co.

1897 Hugh J. McBirney
Assistant Manager National Lead Co.

1897 Alexander A. McCormick

1899 Hiram R. McCullough
Vice-President Chicago & North Western Railway Co.

1896 John J. Mitchell
President Illinois Merchants Trust Co.

1922 James A. Patten

1888 Martin A. Ryerson
134 So. La Salle St.

1899 John A. Spoor
Chairman Board of Directors Union Stock Yards and Transit Co.

1896 Charles L. Strobel
President Strobel Steel Construction Co.

1900 Bernard E. Sunny
Chairman Board of Directors Illinois Bell Telephone Co.

1901 Louis F. Swift
President Swift & Co.

NON-RESIDENT MEMBERS

1896 Nelson P. Bigelow
Bigelow, Arkansas

1896 Richard M. Bissell
Hartford

1895 Robert C. Clowry
New York

1902 Charles R. Crane
New York

1902 Frederic A. Delano
Washington, D. C.

1880 Lyman J. Gage
Point Loma, Cal.

1902 John F. Harris
New York

1898 Charles H. Hodges
Detroit

1902 Edward D. Kenna
New York

1896 William Kent
Kentfield, Cal.

1880 The Right Hon. Lord Leith of Fyvie
Scotland

1898 Robert T. Lincoln
Washington, D. C.

1878 Franklin MacVeagh
Washington, D. C.

1896 John R. Morron
New York

1902 Frank B. Noyes
Washington, D. C.

1902 Edwin A. Potter
New York

1899 James Gamble Rogers
New York

1896 H. Gordon Selfridge
London

1894 Melville E. Stone
New York

DECEASED MEMBERS

Solomon Albert Smith	November, 1879
Edward Swan Stickney	March, 1880
James Monroe Walker	January, 1881
Richard C. Meldrum	April, 1881
George Armour	June, 1881
John Clark Coonley	October, 1882
Charles Palmer Kellogg	April, 1883
Anson Stager	March, 1885
John Winkinson McGenniss	May, 1885
George Clinton Clarke	April, 1887
Martin Ryerson	September, 1887
John Crerar	October, 1889
William Emerson Strong	April, 1891
Uri Balcom	November, 1893
John Burroughs Drake	November, 1895
Charles Mather Henderson	January, 1896
Edson Keith	November, 1896
James Wheeler Oakley	January, 1897
Henry Baldwin Stone	July, 1897
George Mortimer Pullman	October, 1897
Louis Wampold	February, 1898
Henry William King	April, 1898
John DeKoven	April, 1898
William Charles Dustin Grannis	August, 1898
Robert Alexander Waller	February, 1899
George Walker Meeker	April, 1899
Charles Fargo	October, 1900
Philip Danforth Armour	January, 1901
John Wesley Doane	March, 1901
Alexander Caldwell McClurg	April, 1901
John Spragins Hannah	July, 1901
Anthony Frederick Seeberger	July, 1901
John James Janes	August, 1901

Dunlap Smith	December, 1901
Nathaniel Kellogg Fairbank	March, 1903
Charles Benjamin Farwell	September, 1903
William Taylor Baker	October, 1903
William Gold Hibbard	October, 1903
Elias Taylor Watkins	December, 1903
Christoph Hotz	January, 1904
Hermon Beardsley Butler	February, 1904
Eugene Cary	March, 1904
Levi Zeigler Leiter	June, 1904
George Clarke Walker	April, 1905
Elbridge Gerry Keith	May, 1905
Graeme Stewart	June, 1905
Rockwell King	July, 1905
William Chisholm	December, 1905
Marshall Field	January, 1906
William Rainey Harper	January, 1906
Peter Schuttler	September, 1906
James Herron Eckels	April, 1907
Orrin Woodward Potter	May, 1907
John M. Durand	November, 1907
Francis Bolles Peabody	January, 1908
Andrew Brown	August, 1908
Leslie Carter	September, 1908
Charles Frederick Kimball	January, 1909
Otho S. A. Sprague	February, 1909
Charles Leffingwell Bartlett	March, 1909
Turlington W. Harvey	September, 1909
Thomas Murdoch	December, 1909
Henry Homes Porter	March, 1910
Erskine Mason Phelps	May, 1910
James Lawrence Houghteling	July, 1910
Paul Morton	January, 1911
Joseph Tilton Bowen	March, 1911
Augustus Alvord Carpenter	September, 1911

Robert Mather	October, 1911
Richard T. Crane	January, 1912
John W. G. Cofran	January, 1912
Frederick Greeley	January, 1912
James T. Harahan	January, 1912
Daniel H. Burnham	June, 1912
Arthur D. Wheeler	August, 1912
Thies J. Lefens	April, 1913
Clarence Buckingham	August, 1913
Eliphalet W. Blatchford	January, 1914
Byron L. Smith	March, 1914
Franklin H. Head	June, 1914
William S. Warren	August, 1914
Darius Miller	August, 1914
Albert Arnold Sprague	January, 1915
Norman B. Ream	February, 1915
William H. Rand	June, 1915
Edwin G. Foreman	August, 1915
Charles H. Conover	November, 1915
Charles R. Corwith	December, 1915
Henry Baird Favill	February, 1916
Enos M. Barton	May, 1916
William A. Gardner	May, 1916
Murry Nelson	January, 1917
Edward A. Turner	June, 1917
George E. Adams	October, 1917
Homer A. Stillwell	June, 1918
John M. Clark	August, 1918
Harlow N. Higinbotham	April, 1919
Granger Farwell	May, 1919
J. Harley Bradley	June, 1919
La Verne W. Noyes	July, 1919
Edward P. Ripley	February, 1920
Frank H. Armstrong	February, 1920
William Alden Fuller	November, 1920

Henry J. Macfarland . . . . December, 1920
Adolphus C. Bartlett . . . . May, 1922
Rensselaer W. Cox . . . . September, 1922
Charles D. Norton . . . . March, 1923
Edmund D. Hulbert . . . . March, 1923

SUBJECTS OF MEETINGS OF THE COMMERCIAL CLUB OF CHICAGO

1907

George E. Adams, President

April 6.

The City and the State.

RT. HONORABLE JAMES BRYCE, BRITISH AMBASSADOR.

April 27.

CLOSED MEETING.

Plan of Chicago.

1907–1908

John V. Farwell, Jr., President

May 31.

Formal Dinner in honor of General Baron Kuroki.

MAJOR-GENERAL A. W. GREELY, U. S. A., COMMANDER OF THE NORTHERN DIVISION. HONORABLE GEORGE E. ADAMS.

November 9.

The Effect of Industrial Education upon the German Empire.

DR. K. G. RUDOLPH LEONARD, JR., UNIVERSITY OF BRESLAU.

The Effect of Industrial Education upon Labor.

JOHN GOLDEN, PRESIDENT UNITED TEXTILE WORKERS OF AMERICA.

Possibilities of Industrial Education in America.

HENRY S. PRITCHETT, PRESIDENT CARNEGIE FOUNDATION FOR THE ADVANCEMENT OF TEACHING.

December 14.

Public Domain.—Department of the Interior.

HONORABLE ETHAN A. HITCHCOCK, EX-SECRETARY OF THE INTERIOR.

Forestry, Irrigation and Public Lands.

GEORGE H. MAXWELL, EXECUTIVE CHAIRMAN THE NATIONAL IRRIGATION ASSOCIATION.

JANUARY 11.

The Principles of Infection and the Tuberculosis Problem.

DR. L. HEKTOEN, DIRECTOR OF THE MEMORIAL INSTITUTE FOR INFECTIOUS DISEASES.
DR. HENRY BAIRD FAVILL.
DR. FRANK BILLINGS.
DR. WILLIAM A. EVANS, COMMISSIONER OF HEALTH OF CHICAGO.

JANUARY 25.

CLOSED MEETING.

Plan of Chicago.

MARCH 14.

The Government and Business.

WOODROW WILSON, LL. D., PRESIDENT OF PRINCETON UNIVERSITY.

APRIL 4.

Formal Dinner in honor of the Honorable William H. Taft, Secretary of War.

MAY 2.

CLOSED MEETING.

1908–1909

ROLLIN A. KEYES, President

NOVEMBER 3.

Informal Dinner to receive returns of election.

NOVEMBER 14.

The Public Schools of Our Large Cities; Their Administration and Curriculum.

JOHN H. FINLEY, LL. D., PRESIDENT OF THE COLLEGE OF THE CITY OF NEW YORK

DECEMBER 12.

The Psychologist and the Practical Life.

PROFESSOR HUGO MUNSTERBERG OF HARVARD UNIVERSITY.

JANUARY 9.

Parole, Probation and Indeterminate Sentence.

MAJOR R. W. CLAUGHRY OF FT. LEAVENWORTH.
JUDGE ALBERT C. BARNES OF CHICAGO.
JUDGE JULIAN W. MACK OF CHICAGO.
JUDGE CHARLES S. CUTTING OF CHICAGO.

FEBRUARY 13.

The People and the Courts.

MR. EDGAR A. BANCROFT.

APRIL 10.

CLOSED MEETING.

Club guests of Mr. John J. Glessner at his home, 1800 Prairie Avenue.

1909–1910

THEODORE W. ROBINSON, President

JUNE 5.

Formal Dinner in honor of The Honorable Franklin MacVeagh, Secretary of the Treasury, and The Honorable Jacob M. Dickinson, Secretary of War.

SEPTEMBER 16.

Luncheon in honor of William Howard Taft, President of the United States.

NOVEMBER 6.

The Work of the National Monetary Commission.

SENATOR NELSON W. ALDRICH.

JANUARY 8.

The Presentation of the Plan of Chicago.

MR. CHARLES D. NORTON.
MR. CHARLES H. WACKER.
ALDERMAN BERNARD W. SNOW.

FEBRUARY 19.

Employers' Liability and Industrial Insurance.

THE HONORABLE CHARLES NAGEL, SECRETARY OF COMMERCE AND LABOR.
GEORGE M. GILLETTE, MEMBER OF MINNESOTA EMPLOYEES' COMPENSATION COMMISSION.

MARCH 26.

A Federal Immigration Station in Chicago.

SENATOR WILLIAM P. DILLINGHAM, CHAIRMAN OF THE NATIONAL IMMIGRATION COMMISSION.
JUDGE JULIAN W. MACK, PRESIDENT OF THE LEAGUE FOR THE PROTECTION OF IMMIGRANTS.

APRIL 9.

CLOSED MEETING.

1910–1911

DAVID R. FORGAN, President

JUNE 4.

Informal Dinner in honor of The Commercial Club of Cincinnati.

NOVEMBER 12.

CLOSED MEETING: The Commercial Club: Its Past, Present, and Future.

MR. JOHN J. GLESSNER.
MR. FRANK H. JONES.
MR. ALFRED L. BAKER.

DECEMBER 10.

Government of Cities by Commission.

JOHN MACVICAR, MEMBER OF THE COMMISSION GOVERNMENT OF THE CITY OF DES MOINES, IOWA.
H. BALDWIN RICE, MAYOR OF THE CITY OF HOUSTON, TEXAS.
WALTER H. WILSON, COMPTROLLER OF THE CITY OF CHICAGO.

JANUARY 26.

Increasing Cost of Armaments and Rising Cost of Living.

HONORABLE W. BOURKE COCKRAN, OF NEW YORK CITY.

FEBRUARY 25.

The Aldrich Plan for Banking Legislation.

FRANK A. VANDERLIP, PRESIDENT OF THE NATIONAL CITY BANK OF NEW YORK.

APRIL 8.

CLOSED MEETING.

1911-1912

FREDERIC A. DELANO, President

OCTOBER 10.

Exhibition of material on industrial education collected in Europe by Dr. Edwin G. Cooley, Educational Adviser of the Club.

NOVEMBER 11.

Vocational Education.

HERMAN SCHNEIDER, PH. D., DEAN OF THE COLLEGE OF ENGINEERING OF THE UNIVERSITY OF CINCINNATI.

CHARLES H. WINSLOW, SPECIAL AGENT OF THE BUREAU OF LABOR, DEPARTMENT OF COMMERCE AND LABOR.

NOVEMBER 21.

Report on Investigation of Industrial Education in Europe.

EDWIN G. COOLEY, LL. D., EDUCATIONAL ADVISER OF THE CLUB.

Industrial and Technical Education.

MR. RICHARD T. CRANE.

General Discussion.

DECEMBER 9.

CLOSED MEETING.

The Trusts.

MR. ALFRED L. BAKER.

Vocational Education.

MR. WILLIAM L. BROWN

Some Phases of the Club's Activity in the Work of Its Committees.

MR. CLYDE M. CARR.

Optimism.

MR. JOHN J. GLESSNER.

The Welfare of Chicago.

MR. CHARLES L. HUTCHINSON.

Public Service Corporations.

MR. SAMUEL INSULL.

Currency Legislation and Currency Reform.

MR. GEORGE M. REYNOLDS.

Co-operation.

MR. JOHN W. SCOTT.

Business.

MR. LOUIS F. SWIFT.

Industrial Insurance.

MR. CHARLES H. THORNE.

JANUARY 13.

The Welfare of the Children.

How to Prevent Delinquency.

MRS. JOSEPH T. BOWEN, PRESIDENT OF THE JUVENILE PROTECTIVE ASSOCIATION.

The Funds to Parents Act and How to Treat Delinquency.

HON. MERRITT W. PINCKNEY, CHIEF JUSTICE OF THE CIRCUIT COURT OF COOK COUNTY AND JUDGE OF THE JUVENILE COURT.

FEBRUARY 10.

CLOSED MEETING.

The Trust Problem.

MR. EDGAR A. BANCROFT.

Taxation.

MR. ADOLPHUS C. BARTLETT.

The Lake Front Improvement.

MR. EDWARD B. BUTLER.

Supervision of the Trusts.

MR. DAVID R. FORGAN.

Industrial Education.

MR. THEODORE W. ROBINSON.

The Panama Canal.

MR. JOHN E. WILDER.

MARCH 16.

Education for National Efficiency.

GEORGE E. VINCENT, LL. D., PRESIDENT OF THE UNIVERSITY OF MINNESOTA.

APRIL 13.

CLOSED MEETING.

Discussion of Reform of Taxation in Illinois.

1912–1913

CLYDE M. CARR, President

MAY 6.

Report of Committee Appointed to Consider the Advisability of the Club Taking Action Looking to the Reform of Revenue Laws of the State of Illinois.

NOVEMBER 9.

Necessary Reforms in the System of State Taxation in Illinois.

Why There is Urgent Need of Reform.
MR. JOHN P. WILSON.

Fundamental Condition of Achieving Reform.
DR. EDMUND J. JAMES, PRESIDENT UNIVERSITY OF ILLINOIS.

Necessary Changes in Administration to Secure Permanent Reform.
MR. HARRISON B. RILEY, PRESIDENT CHICAGO TITLE & TRUST COMPANY.

DECEMBER 14.

What is Progress in Politics?
DR. NICHOLAS MURRAY BUTLER, PRESIDENT COLUMBIA UNIVERSITY.

JANUARY 11.

The Business Future of the Country.
GOVERNOR WOODROW WILSON,
President-Elect of the United States.

FEBRUARY 8.

CLOSED MEETING.

Federal Immigration Station in Chicago.
MR. JOHN E. WILDER.

Revision of Illinois Taxation Laws.
MR. BERNARD A. ECKHART.

Vocational Education.
MR. CLAYTON MARK.
MR. EDWIN G. COOLEY.
MR. EDWARD F. CARRY.
MR. ALLEN B. POND.

Plan of Chicago.

MR. EDWARD B. BUTLER.

Stereopticon Lecture.

MR. WALTER D. MOODY.

MARCH 8.

The Department of the Interior.

HON. WALTER L. FISHER, SECRETARY THE DEPARTMENT OF THE INTERIOR.

Stereopticon Views and Moving Pictures Illustrative of the Scope and Work of The Department of the Interior.

MR. C. J. BLANCHARD, OF THE RECLAMATION SERVICE.

APRIL 25.

CLOSED MEETING.

Plan of Chicago.

Revision of Illinois Taxation Laws.

Federal Immigration Station in Chicago.

Vocational Education.

1913–1914

BENJAMIN CARPENTER, President

NOVEMBER 8.

The Diplomatic and Consular Service of the United States.

HON. WILLIAM J. CALHOUN, FORMER MINISTER TO CHINA.

DECEMBER 13.

The Meeting Ground of Business and Philanthropy.

E. R. L. GOULD, PH. D., LL. D., PRESIDENT CITY AND SUBURBAN HOMES COMPANY, NEW YORK.

FEBRUARY 14.

The Public Utility and the Public.

MORTIMER E. COOLEY, LL. D., ENG. D., DEAN, DEPARTMENT OF ENGINEERING, UNIVERSITY OF MICHIGAN.

HON. OWEN P. THOMPSON OF THE STATE PUBLIC UTILITIES COMMISSION OF ILLINOIS.

MARCH 14.

CLOSED MEETING.

The American Academy in Rome.

DR. JESSE BENEDICT CARTER, DIRECTOR OF THE AMERICAN ACADEMY IN ROME.

APRIL 11.

CLOSED MEETING.

Federal Immigration Station in Chicago.

Plan of Chicago.

Vocational Education.

1914–1915

BERNARD E. SUNNY, President

OCTOBER 12.

Formal Dinner in honor of John V. Farwell, President of the National Citizens' League for the Promotion of a Sound Banking System, and Frederic A. Delano, Vice-Governor Federal Reserve Board.

MR. JAMES B. FORGAN.
MR. HARRY A. WHEELER.
PROF. J. LAURENCE LAUGHLIN.
MR. JOHN V. FARWELL.
MR. GEORGE M. REYNOLDS.
MR. EDGAR A. BANCROFT.
MR. CHARLES G. DAWES.
MR. FREDERIC A. DELANO.

NOVEMBER 20.

Economy and Efficiency in Government.

WILLIAM HOWARD TAFT, LL. D.

DECEMBER 12.

The Urgent Need for a Federal Budget.

DR. WILLIAM H. ALLEN.

JANUARY 9.

The Shipping Bill as a Means for the Development and Expansion of our Merchant Marine.

HON. WILLIAM G. MCADOO, SECRETARY OF THE TREASURY.

February 13.

CLOSED MEETING.

Chicago Plan Commission.

MR. CHARLES H. WACKER.

Vocational Education.

MR. THEODORE W. ROBINSON.

Revision of Illinois Taxation Laws.

MR. BERNARD A. ECKHART.

Federal Budget.

MR. HARRY A. WHEELER.

March 13.

Some History and Some Questions.

HENRY DODGE ESTABROOK, ESQ.

April 10.

CLOSED MEETING.

Plan of Chicago.

Vocational Education.

Revision of Illinois Taxation Laws.

1915–1916

John W. Scott, President

September 28.

Formal dinner in honor of The Right Honorable Lord Chief Justice of England.

HON. CHARLES S. CUTTING.
BARON READING OF ERLEIGH, LORD CHIEF JUSTICE OF ENGLAND.
M. ERNEST MALLETT.

November 13.

CLOSED MEETING.

Plan of Chicago.

MR. CHARLES H. WACKER.

State Budget and Efficiency.

MR. MEDILL McCORMICK.

Military Preparedness and Training Camps.

MR. HENRY H. PORTER.

Discussion of By-Laws.

DECEMBER 13.

Military Instruction Camps.

Citizen Training Camps.

MAJOR GENERAL LEONARD WOOD, U. S. A.

JANUARY 8.

CLOSED MEETING.

State Budget and Efficiency.

MR. HOMER A. STILLWELL.

General Discussion, Daniels Correspondence.

FEBRUARY 12.

The Trilogy of Democracy.

DARWIN P. KINGSLEY, ESQ., OF NEW YORK.

MARCH 11.

CLOSED MEETING.

Institute for Government Research.

DR. FREDERICK A. CLEVELAND, DIRECTOR OF THE BUREAU OF MUNICIPAL RESEARCH, NEW YORK CITY.

MR. RAYMOND B. FOSDICK, SECRETARY INSTITUTE FOR GOVERNMENT RESEARCH.

APRIL 8.

CLOSED MEETING.

1916–1917

JAMES B. FORGAN, President

APRIL 27.

Military Preparedness.

BRIGADIER GENERAL FRANK S. DICKSON.
COLONEL JOSEPH B. SANBORN.
COLONEL MILTON J. FOREMAN.
CAPTAIN EDWARD A. EVERS.

NOVEMBER 11.

Proceedings and Procedure in Congress.

CONGRESSMAN JAMES R. MANN.

DECEMBER 9.

Views on Military Preparedness as Modified by Texas Campaign.

MAJOR ABEL DAVIS, ILLINOIS NATIONAL GUARD.
COLONEL MILTON J. FOREMAN, ILLINOIS NATIONAL GUARD.

JANUARY 13.

Work of Federal Trade Commission.

HONORABLE EDWARD N. HURLEY, CHAIRMAN OF THE COMMISSION.

FEBRUARY 10.

Military Training in Camps and Schools.

MAJOR GENERAL THOMAS H. BARRY, U. S. A.
MAJOR PAUL B. MALONE, U. S. A.
CAPTAIN EDGAR Z. STEEVER, U. S. A.

APRIL 7.

Government and Business.

HONORABLE PAUL M. WARBURG, VICE-GOVERNOR, FEDERAL RESERVE BOARD, WASHINGTON, D. C.

MAY 5.

CLOSED MEETING.

Consideration of reports of Officers and Committees for Club Year 1916–17.

1917–1918

HARRISON B. RILEY, President

NOVEMBER 10.

Financial and Economic Relations of the United States and Japan.

BARON TENETARO MEGATA AND THE SPECIAL FINANCE COMMISSION FROM JAPAN.

DECEMBER 8.

The Problems of the War.

HONORABLE MEDILL McCORMICK.

JANUARY 5.

Business Problems During and After the War.

JUDGE ELBERT H. GARY.

FEBRUARY 16.

Ideals of the World War.

SIR WALTER ROPER LAWRENCE.

MARCH 9.

The Centennial Year.

HONORABLE FRANK O. LOWDEN, GOVERNOR OF THE STATE OF ILLINOIS.

APRIL 20.

CLOSED MEETING.

Consideration of reports of Officers and Committees for Club Year 1917–1918.

1918–1919

THOMAS E. DONNELLEY, President

NOVEMBER 9.

The Commercial Club and the War.

MR. THOMAS E. DONNELLEY.
MR. STANLEY FIELD.
MR. DAVID R. FORGAN.
MR. SAMUEL M. FELTON.

DECEMBER 14.

The Future of Industry.

MR. FREDERICK P. FISH, CHAIRMAN NATIONAL INDUSTRIAL CONFERENCE BOARD.

JANUARY 18.

Illinois in the War.

HONORABLE FRANK O. LOWDEN, GOVERNOR OF THE STATE OF ILLINOIS.
MR. SAMUEL INSULL, CHAIRMAN OF THE STATE COUNCIL OF DEFENSE.

FEBRUARY 8.

CLOSED MEETING.

The Commercial Club and the War.

MR. JULIUS ROSENWALD.
MR. CYRUS H. McCORMICK.
MR. ROBERT P. LAMONT.
MR. H. M. BYLLESBY.
MR. JOHN W. SCOTT.

MARCH 8.

One Way Out of the Railroad Dilemma.

MR. HOWARD ELLIOTT, PRESIDENT NORTHERN PACIFIC RAILWAY COMPANY.

Two Years of Effort.

MRS. JOSEPH T. BOWEN, STATE CHAIRMAN OF THE WOMAN'S COMMITTEE, COUNCIL OF NATIONAL DEFENSE, ILLINOIS DIVISION.

APRIL 12.

CLOSED MEETING.

Consideration of Reports of Officers and Committees for Club Year 1918–1919.

Annual Election.

1919–1920

EDGAR A. BANCROFT, President

*APRIL 23.—Special Meeting. The Commercial Club of Chicago and The Industrial Club of Chicago.

The Merchant Marine:

CAPTAIN ROBERT DOLLAR OF SAN FRANCISCO.
MR. HOMER L. FERGUSON OF NEWPORT NEWS.

JUNE 14.—Special Meeting.

The Lessons of the War as to Universal Military Training.

COLONEL JOSEPH B. SANBORN.
COLONEL MILTON J. FOREMAN.
COLONEL HENRY J. REILLY.
COLONEL HENRY A. ALLEN.
COLONEL ABEL DAVIS.
COLONEL JOHN V. CLINNIN.

NOVEMBER 15.

Some Needs of Chicago.

MAJOR GENERAL WILLIAM M. BLACK, Late Chief of Engineers United States Army, Chairman of the Port and Harbor Facilities Commission.

DECEMBER 6.—Special Closed Meeting.

The State Militia.

HONORABLE FRANK O. LOWDEN, GOVERNOR OF THE STATE OF ILLINOIS.

*Included in Year Book, 1918–1919.

JANUARY 10.

CLOSED MEETING.

Crime Conditions in Chicago.

MR. MACLAY HOYNE.
MR. ALFRED S. AUSTRIAN.

FEBRUARY 14.

The Constitutional Convention.

HON. ORRIN N. CARTER, JUDGE OF THE SUPREME COURT OF THE STATE OF ILLINOIS.

The Duty of the Citizen with Respect to the Constitutional Convention.

MR. SILAS H. STRAWN.

MARCH 13.

Mineral Resources in their International Relation.

DR. C. K. LEITH, MINERAL ADVISER TO THE WAR BOARDS, WASHINGTON, AND TO THE AMERICAN PEACE COMMISSION, PARIS.

APRIL 10.

CLOSED MEETING.

Consideration of reports of Officers and Committees for Club Year 1919–1920.

Annual Election.

1920–1921

HOWARD ELTING, President

JANUARY 27.

CLOSED MEETING.

Economy in Governmental Expenditures and Reduced Taxation.

GENERAL CHARLES G. DAWES

FEBRUARY 21.

CLOSED MEETING.

Conditions in Europe.

UNITED STATES SENATOR MEDILL McCORMICK

MARCH 16.

The Situation in England.

MR. HARRY GORDON SELFRIDGE OF LONDON, ENGLAND

MARCH 28.

Canadian Potentialities.

SIR GEORGE EULAS FOSTER, MINISTER OF TRADE AND COMMERCE, DOMINION OF CANADA, AND CANADA'S REPRESENTATIVE AT THE PEACE CONFERENCE IN 1919.

APRIL 29.

CLOSED MEETING.

Consideration of reports of Officers and Committees for Club Year 1920-1921.

Annual Election.

1921–1922

SAMUEL INSULL, President

MAY 18, 1921.—Special Meeting.

DINNER IN HONOR OF THE RIGHT HONORABLE SIR AUCKLAND CAMPBELL GEDDES, K.C.B., BRITISH AMBASSADOR TO THE UNITED STATES.

OCTOBER 25, 1921.—Special Meeting.

International Trade and Finance.

RIGHT HONORABLE REGINALD MCKENNA, CHAIRMAN OF THE LONDON JOINT CITY AND MIDLAND BANK, LIMITED, AND FORMERLY CHANCELLOR OF THE EXCHEQUER.

NOVEMBER 3, 1921.

DINNER IN HONOR OF THE RIGHT HONORABLE ADMIRAL OF THE FLEET THE EARL BEATTY, FIRST SEA LORD OF THE BRITISH ADMIRALTY.

DECEMBER 9, 1921.

CLOSED MEETING.

JANUARY 21, 1922.

Some of Our Problems.

MR. MELVILLE E. STONE OF NEW YORK.

MARCH 4, 1922.

Why I Believe in a Community Fund.

MR. FRED W. RAMSEY, PRESIDENT OF THE CLEVELAND METAL PRODUCTS COMPANY, CHAIRMAN OF CAMPAIGN COMMITTEE, CLEVELAND COMMUNITY FUND.

APRIL 17, 1922.

DINNER IN HONOR OF MARSHAL JOFFRE OF FRANCE.

MAY 17, 1922.

CLOSED MEETING.

CONSIDERATION OF REPORTS OF OFFICERS AND COMMITTEES FOR CLUB YEAR 1921-1922.

Annual Election.

1922-1923

BERNARD E. SUNNY, President

NOVEMBER 17, 1922.

The Railroad Situation.

MR. SAMUEL REA, PRESIDENT THE PENNSYLVANIA RAILROAD SYSTEM.

DECEMBER 8, 1922.

The Foreign Trade Outlook.

MR. JULIUS H. BARNES, PRESIDENT UNITED STATES CHAMBER OF COMMERCE.

American Ships for Foreign Trade.

CAPTAIN WILLIAM H. STAYTON, PRESIDENT BALTIMORE STEAMSHIP COMPANY.

JANUARY 13, 1923.

Labor, Immigration and Citizenship.

HONORABLE JAMES J. DAVIS, SECRETARY OF LABOR.

FEBRUARY 9, 1923.

CLOSED MEETING.

MARCH 9, 1923.

World Communications.

BRIGADIER GENERAL JOHN J. CARTY, VICE-PRESIDENT IN CHARGE OF THE DEVELOPMENT AND RESEARCH OF THE AMERICAN TELEGRAPH & TELEPHONE COMPANY.

APRIL 13, 1923.

CLOSED MEETING.

RESIDENCE OF BERNARD E. SUNNY.

Consideration of reports of officers and committees for Club Year 1922–1923.
Annual Election.

NOTE

(From Year-Book of 1909)

The list of meetings and subjects gives only an inadequate idea of the activities of The Commercial Club and The Merchants Club, but indicates that they have extended over municipal, state, and national affairs, and have included governmental, commercial and educational, moral, charitable and esthetic subjects.

For many years The Commercial Club confined its efforts to discussions and suggestions, with a distinct policy not to take up and, as a Club, conduct any particular work, and only occasionally has it departed from this policy.

Of the two hundred and eighty-three meetings that have been held by the two Clubs, it is within bounds to say that each one has helped to forward some good end, and many of them have been the initial and moving causes of important accomplishments. It would be invidious and almost impossible to estimate the relative value of these meetings or say which was the most important, bearing in mind that, in any great permanent work, the prime necessity is for forming public opinion before there can be any accomplishment.

Perhaps the meetings from which The Commercial Club's influence was most directly and speedily felt were those that resulted in founding the Chicago Manual Training School; in presenting to the United States Government the site for Fort Sheridan, and, to the State, the site for the Second Regiment Armory; in the prosecution and punishment of certain county and municipal officials; in the original efforts for legislation for the Drainage Canal;

in its early advocacy and support of the World's Columbian Exposition; in raising endowment funds for the Illinois Manual Training School at Glenwood and the St. Charles School for Boys; also in presenting to the city a site for public playgrounds at Chicago Avenue and Lincoln Street. The meetings from which The Merchants Club's influence was most directly felt were those that resulted in establishing the First State Pawners' Society; in the inquiry into the City's accounting methods that resulted in new and improved systems; and most of all, in its earnest efforts to amend the general school law in order to provide improvements in the system of public education; and in the inception and development of the Chicago Plan, which work was later continued by the united Commercial Club and Merchants Club. The joint effort of both Clubs resulted in presenting to the United States Government a site for the Naval Training School at Lake Bluff, and in establishing a street cleaning bureau for the City.

These and other philanthropic and public-spirited works of these two Clubs, now merged into one, have involved the collection and disbursement of more than a million of dollars, and have been potent in many reforms and improvements.

TWO HUNDRED AND EIGHTY-SECOND REGULAR MEETING

THE BLACKSTONE

FRIDAY, NOVEMBER 17, 1922.

Open Meeting: President B. E. Sunny Presiding

Invocation: Reverend Frederick F. Shannon

AN ADDRESS:

THE RAILROAD SITUATION

AND

THE PENNSYLVANIA RAILWAY SYSTEM

MR. SAMUEL REA

President The Pennsylvania Railway System

PRESIDENT SUNNY: President Rea, fellow members of the Commercial Club, guests: I extend to you a very sincere and cordial welcome to this first meeting of the Commercial Club in this club year of 1922–23, and I am very glad that we have a topic to discuss tonight which I know will interest you all.

There are many hundreds of steam railroads in the United States with their separate properties, their separate stockholders, officers and employes, all independent of each other in a corporate way, but under the Federal laws and regulations, as operating utilities, they substantially constitute a single system. The value of the properties that they own, the number of men and women that they employ, and the territory and the people that they serve is so great that in the aggregate they constitute one of the largest operating utilities in all the world—larger, indeed, in property employed and persons employed than in the case of the Federal Government and all of the state governments combined, and with reference to their activities on the prosperity and happiness of the people, they are equal to government itself.

There is no other business that has the responsibility continuously for the safety of so many lives, and such a large amount of valuable property; therefore the personnel must be, and as a matter of fact is, of long experience, unquestioned skill and the highest ability.

Railroad history, particularly during the past few years, has been unsatisfactory, and basic questions of management and operation have been constantly before the public, and have been a source of great disturbance to the general business.

Furthermore, the results of the recent election are interpreted in some quarters as indicating probable additional legislation disadvantageous to the railroads. We are justified in feeling serious concern about this proposition, because the record proves that the greatest development in our steam railways was at a time when the Government had the least control in their affairs, and as such control or direction has increased, development has fallen off.

In the nature of things, this result might have been anticipated. Our efforts to increase the efficiency of Government have not succeeded, because of the inherent difficulties due to a constantly changing personnel, and the inexperience of the incoming officials. Omissions and failures in governmental operations are commonplace, and we are fortunate that they seldom affect us immediately or directly.

On the other hand, omissions or failures in railroad operation do affect us directly and immediately. If the railway stops, everything stops.

It is therefore extremely unfortunate that we have selected, to direct the vital affairs of a delicately organized, technical and highly efficient public service, an agency which, in more than a hundred years, has failed to establish a reputation for efficiency in its own operations!

There are magnificent properties in this great system,—properties that appeal to our admiration and pride, and which in management, construction and operation, are the very best expression of all that is known in the art,—among them the Pennsylvania Railroad, which has a record of seventy-five years of honorable achievement in the service of the public.

The Pennsylvania, the conquerer of the Alleghenies, represents the work of the engineer to a larger degree than is ordinarily the case with a railroad property, and its executives have generally risen from the ranks of the engineering corps,—starting as rodmen, or in some other humble capacity, and, by industry, loyalty and ability, advancing from one position to another of increasing importance and responsibility, until they have finally ranked at the top.

Our distinguished guest on this occasion, the ninth President of this great corporation, acquired his high office in orthodox fashion, beginning as chainman and rodman fifty-one years ago, and successively filling the positions of Assistant Engineer, Engineer, Assistant to Second Vice-President, Assistant to the President, Fourth, Third, Second and First Vice-President, and finally ten years ago receiving appointment to the Presidency.

He is the successor of men of acknowledged genius, energy, diplomacy, far-sightedness, lofty ideals and patriotism, among them Colonel Tom Scott, who, as Assistant Secretary of War, was one of Lincoln's most dependable helpers in connection with the railways and the telegraph in the darkest days of the Civil War.

Mr. Rea's term of office has been at a time of severest stress and peril, not only with reference to the Pennsylvania Railroad, but to our country, and he has discharged the responsibility of his position with consummate skill. The best traditions of the Pennsylvania have been maintained, and he has amply and fully measured up to the ability and achievements of the great men who have preceded him.

I have the very great pleasure now to present our guest of the evening, Mr. Samuel Rea, President of the Pennsylvania Railroad.

THE RAILROAD SITUATION:

ADDRESS BY

MR. SAMUEL REA

President The Pennsylvania Railroad System

MR. CHAIRMAN AND GENTLEMEN: I regard it a rare opportunity as a member of the railroad profession to be invited to talk to you in this intimate fashion. What I have to say on the railroad situation I hope to do earnestly and sincerely, and therefore, in order that I shall not make any mistakes in the message which I have to convey to you, I shall have to ask your pardon for adhering pretty closely to my notes.

THE PENNSYLVANIA RAILROAD SYSTEM

It is a great pleasure, and a great responsibility as well, to address you on the railroad situation at present, and try to give you a glimpse of the Pennsylvania System and of the future of the transportation industry as a whole as I view it. As many of you travel on the Pennsylvania Railroad, and I hope read its dining car menus, it needs but few words to tell you that the Pennsylvania Railroad System plays a very important part in railroad transportation—equal to about 11 per cent of the entire freight transportation service, and about 17 per cent of the passenger service of the whole country. It is a great national highway for trade and transportation. The Pennsylvania System represents an investment of over two billion two hundred million dollars. Its total outstanding bonds and stocks amount at par to over $1,950,000,000, of which only $1,420,000,000 are held by the public, and the balance is held by the Pennsylvania Railroad Company itself and the subsidiary companies in its System, as a means of unifying the System until finally we can compact it into one operating company. We have a railroad property directly owned by the citizens in all walks of life, and their institutions, totaling close to 140,000 stockholders and many thousands of bondholders.

For over three-quarters of a century this company has paid a moderate cash dividend in every calendar year. The foundation for its ability to pay such dividends in good and bad periods has been its conservative capital structure, to which I have just referred. That structure was built on our recognized policy, by which the income above these moderate dividends, and the income derived from investments over this long period of its existence, were put back into the property for the improvement and development for transportation service, when legitimately such profits might have been paid as dividends. It paid 6 per cent cash dividends on the capital stock for many years, because so many hundred millions of dollars of income were invested in the property in past years and no securities were issued against the same. We have just increased the quarterly dividend from 1 per cent, to which we were forced in 1921, to 1½ per cent, making the total dividend disbursed to the stockholders in 1922 equal to 4½ per cent. So many stockholders and institutions and industries are dependent on the prosperity of the Company that you can readily understand the desire of our Directors and Management to continue the dividend at the rate of 6 per cent per annum. We wish to retain the present body of stockholders, and have the basis of credit to obtain the capital essential for the future development of the System.

CHICAGO

You have the greatest evidence in the very costly grade crossing eliminations and track elevations, and the large and expensive area dedicated to passenger and freight station facilities, that Chicago has had a very generous share of our capital expenditures and of transportation service. We recognize Chicago as a great railroad, business and navigation center, and as the greatest mid-continental, agricultural, mercantile and transportation exchange in the United States, for which we were willing to do even more if we had had the available resources. With this brief introduction I will pass from Chicago and the Pennsylvania System to the railroad situation as a whole.

THE PRESENT RAILROAD SITUATION

The railroads of the United States, in the closing quarter of the present eventful year, face an array of unusual and in some respects unprecedented difficulties. It is extremely important that the facts of the situation be thoroughly grasped by shippers, travelers, and the public generally.

Since the close of 1921 there has been a reversal of business conditions in America, and with all the hard knocks it is a change for the better. From extreme dullness we have rapidly advanced to a point where railroad traffic is close to record levels.

SERIOUS CONGESTION AND ITS CAUSES

The situation is more difficult to handle now than during the war, when individual conveniences and advantages were patriotically sacrificed. Grave congestion exists which I trust will be short-lived, and many emergency measures are being used, so as to relieve the situation. The immediate causes are: (1) the resumption of coal mining after a suspension of some five months, which was complete in the anthracite regions, and affected a large majority of the bituminous mines. In the few weeks before winter descends upon the more northern portions of the country, it is necessary to handle a coal traffic for domestic, railroad and industrial uses ordinarily spread over months, but I think that so far as the bituminous coal is concerned, we have measurably met the situation; (2) the flood of general business, partly to restore long existing shortages in building and other lines, and partly due to the sudden resumption of activity in those branches of trade which were curtailed, or stopped during the coal strike; (3) the enormous crops of the present year, which in many cases break all previous records and are now coming to market in maximum quantities; and (4) the depression in 1921, when the railroads could not earn sufficient to maintain all their cars and engines, and, before that could be done, we had the general shopmen's strike.

You cannot dam the current of millions of tons of coal, crops and industrial output for months in 1922; make up the bad condition of equipment following the release of the railroads from Federal control and the depression of 1921, and deal with a shopmen's strike, and expect transportation service to be satisfactory. Railroad men are struggling to make it so, but even if the railroads were in the best of condition, with a full complement of engines and cars, and had enjoyed fair profits for a number of years and had ample facilities and full opportunity for preparation, the situation would be a most difficult one to handle. But other causes, more deeply rooted and dangerous, have helped to produce this undesirable situation. Among the most important of these may be mentioned the following:

LONG UNREMUNERATIVE RETURNS THE CHIEF CAUSE OF CONGESTION

The political attacks on railroads, followed by restrictive and repressive regulations by Federal and State bodies, the pressure for reduced rates, and the ruinously low investment returns allowed the railroads for over a dozen years, have kept railroad development in this country below normal requirements in new lines, yards, equipment and facilities. The low returns likewise have made it impossible to finance these necessities through the sale of capital stock or even of bonds.

SLOW GOVERNMENT SETTLEMENTS HURTFUL

Delayed settlement by the Government of the compensation for the war-time use of the railroads during Federal control and the guaranty periods ending August, 1920, created several financial obstacles in the way of restoring the general physical condition of the railroads and the equipment from the wear and tear of the war. In fairness I must say that the present officers of the Government and the Interstate Commerce Commission are doing what they can to hasten settlements which even now would be constructive help.

REDUCED FREIGHT RATES PREMATURE

On and even before July 1 of this year, freight rates were reduced 10 per cent, some of them by voluntary action of the railroads in the hope that it would stimulate general business and assist in deflating war costs, but the reduction further curtailed the resources of the railroad companies, because the war-time railroad wages and working conditions have been but slightly deflated, and fuel, taxes, and other costs have increased greatly in 1922, due to the strikes and other conditions.

In effect the railroads were hurt while business generally was returning good profits, and thereby the railroads were further crippled in their efforts to provide transportation.

DIFFICULTIES OF TRAFFIC PEAKS AND DEPRESSIONS

I think the public should bear in mind that the necessity of handling an extremely fluctuating volume of traffic imposes upon our railroads practical difficulties of a character which most other forms of business do not feel in anything like equal degree. The capacity of a railroad, i.e., its tracks, yards, stations, cars and locomotives, and those of the systems with which it connects, must, in order to avoid long periods of congestion, be fairly adequate for the handling of peak traffic, although "peaks" are of brief duration and occur only for a short period in each year.

Manufacturing industries are, of course, subject to "peaks" and depressions, but the manufacturer can anticipate the future or close down for a time if the interests of the business so require. A railroad, however, cannot shut down, nor can transportation be manufactured in advance. A railroad company must accept traffic, and should be able to perform the service immediately when offered, or, practically, it fails to function.

Some idea of what these violent swings mean may be gained from the fact that in the last nine months alone the number of loaded freight cars handled per week on the Pennsylvania Railroad System has been as low as 96,000 and as high as 180,000. In the week ended November 4, the Pennsylvania Railroad System moved nearly 19 per cent more loaded cars than in 1921, and 11 per cent over 1920, so you see we are alive to the situation, because this has been accomplished without any material increase of equipment or facilities.

HIGH COSTS OF CAR SHORTAGES

It is idle to waste time on mere complaint; it does not help us nor the public; so we are endeavoring to give the best possible service, improve facilities and order new equipment. But it is inevitable that the railroads now have more traffic offered to them than their available facilities can handle in the normal way and with reasonable promptness. The situation, present and prospective, as between the railroads and patrons, is one that calls in the highest degree for mutual understanding, patience, tact and helpfulness. The co-operation of patrons in such matters as the prompt loading and unloading of all cars, and the loading of all cars as far as possible to maximum capacity—practices which have been so helpful in past emergencies—are now urgently required.

With these aids, upon which the railroad executives confidently count, I hope it will be possible during this critical period to measurably furnish the country with its necessary transportation and avoid long congestion and confusion. Such congestions or so-called "car shortages" are costly to our people. The Honorable Herbert Hoover is reported to have stated recently that he believed such congestions cost the country over a billion dollars, while Mr. Julius Barnes, President of the United States Chamber of Commerce, estimates that it has cost the farmers a loss of $400,000,000. They are both unanimous in the opinion that the railroad business is hurt by over-regulation.

WHAT CAN REMEDY THE SITUATION?

But you will ask, is there no remedy for this situation? Must the railroad investors, the business men, the farmers and the country suffer this condition to continue and concur in the gradual paralysis of their own business and individual initiative? What will mitigate the burden and enable the country to gradually work back again to ample transportation service? Just begin by telling your State and National Representatives and Senators to stop tinkering with the railroads, as they will not be saved by legislation, but by freedom to manage their properties under minimum reasonable regulation and to earn a fair return. If they fail to earn it your business is hurt and your business costs and living costs are increased.

GOVERNMENT OWNERSHIP AND OPERATION A RUINOUS EXPERIMENT

But some offhand observers will say, let us try Government ownership, and have the taxpayers brought into the situation to pay the bill by assuming the additional cost of sustaining the $20,000,000,000 railroad investment of the country, and of providing about $1,000,000,000 of new capital annually to keep it abreast of the traffic demands. There is no comfort to be found in the politicalization of the railroads, their employes, and wages and rates, nor in losing a source which now pays the State and National Governments over $285,000,000 a year in taxes, as the railroads are doing. There can be no expectation that the political parties will adopt and adhere to a continuously constructive and non-partisan policy for the railroads and the business interests of the country. I ask you to look into Government operation at home or abroad. Most of its originators mean well and start well, but ultimately it results not in business-like Government ownership and operation, but in political partisan operation; political wage adjustments to appease labor; delay in demanding fair rates so as not to displease the public; bureaucracy and expediency that produce large deficits, which business men and citizens who work and save money, must pay in additional taxation.

FAILURE OF STATE TRANSPORTATION IN PENNSYLVANIA AND ELSEWHERE

I would like to call your attention to the disastrous experiment in State ownership and operation right in my own home state of Pennsylvania, which was the first to complete its "Public Works," consisting of rail and canal transportation across the State of Pennsylvania between tidewater at Philadelphia and the head-waters of the Ohio River at Pittsburgh, a distance of about 395 miles. I came into the world just as the failing experiment was ended, that is, about 1855, but I was cognizant of the aftermath of what really proved to be a disastrous experiment by the State, both ethically and financially, although, of course, the State received some benefit from this twenty-year experiment through the development of its industries and increased population.

The State of Pennsylvania lost, all told, on its canals and railroads, over $50,000,000, and when the end of political operation came, including patronage-free transportation, which ran riot, not to mention the corruption incident to furnishing supplies, the State was glad to sell all its Public Works, lock, stock and barrel, to the Pennsylvania Railroad, which had been granted the right to build a railroad supplementing that part of the Public Works between Harrisburg and Pittsburgh. That ruinous result was not desired, but experience demonstrated that the railroads owned by the citizens and operated by them were a much more expeditious and cheaper method of transportation than canals. Railroads are not stopped by weather or physical difficulties, they carry traffic without transfer from mine to mill and from the manufacturer or the harvest fields direct to the consumers. That is the situation today, notwithstanding all efforts to subsidize waterways, roads or canals. Other illustrations of Government railroads could be cited, such as the experience in Italy and other countries, and coming closer to home I might mention Canada, where the huge deficits in the operation of the Canadian National System have brought about 50 per cent of the railroad mileage of that great country to the verge of bankruptcy, and must be sustained by the taxpayer or shut down in whole or in part.

FEDERAL OPERATION DEMORALIZING

We had our own experience with unrestricted Government operation during the war period under the best of conditions for making it a success, namely, a patriotic public, and railroad managements determined that the war should be won and our country saved; all the railroad facilities and equipment pooled; a maximum volume of traffic and unlimited capital resources at the command of the Government to purchase new equipment and construct additional facilities; and with unlimited means to pay the high wages and give the most liberal working conditions, to secure the best results from what ought to have been a satisfied body of men. You and the railroad owners and managers know the results of this experiment better than I can tell you. Promises or contracts did not prevent the roads and equipment from being returned in poor condition, with large capital debts, their operating forces demoralized, cars scattered all over the country, the rates absolutely unprofitable and the wages and working conditions needing immediate readjustment.

PUBLIC CO-OPERATION IN CAR LOADING AND UNLOADING

We must, therefore, reject the idea that our changing form of Government can get better business results than the citizens themselves, and must rely not so much upon tinkering with governmental laws or regulation, but on our own initiative and loyalty to the public, who trust us with their investments and expect a well-managed transportation system, and with informed and organized public co-operation and opinion try to make the best out of what we have, so as to enable the railroads to earn a fair return, to produce good service for the public and steady employment and fair wages for the employes.

This public opinion with avoidance of all panic or unwise speculation, or hoarding of products or fuel, and with active public co-operation in loading and unloading cars so as to multiply their usefulness, is the first step to mitigate the present obstacles.

AVOID LEGISLATIVE TINKERING WITH THE RAILROADS

Unfortunately the farms, the mines, the industries and the traveling public, and even railroad employes must suffer some of the delay and loss which comes from such long-continued destructive and restrictive laws, from strikes and a public policy that for so long denied fair rates, heaped up operating costs and taxes, and prevented a proper return on the cost of their road and equipment, and forced the public to invest its money in other channels. But we will suffer even more if we allow the wreckers of the constructive forces of the country to further tinker with a great business enterprise like our transportation system.

Take the allegations that railroads are over-capitalized and that rates were, and are, too high. The frequent repetition of this statement eventually forced the Federal Act of 1913 to value the railroads, and also the Transportation Act of 1920 to limit rates so as to produce a return of 5¾ per cent, but with no guarantee whatever that the railroads would earn even that modest return.

However, as contrasted with preceding punitive regulation, the Federal Transportation Act in 1920 was intended to be a helpful step in the solution of the railroad situation. The carrying out of several of its provisions is based upon the valuation work of the Interstate Commerce Commission, authorized by the Act of 1913. After almost ten years' work in this great joint economic undertaking, at a cost to the Government of over $23,000,000, and to the railroads of nearly $65,000,000, only several hundred tentative valuations of the smaller roads, and three or four of the larger roads have been announced by the Interstate Commerce Commission, which so far has not stated the principles of their determination of value to the public, or to railroad owners and managers. It is now evident that the book value of the railroads as a whole will be sustained, that the alleged over-capitalization is fiction, taking the investment as a whole. When such laws are passed, the Interstate Commerce Commission and the railroads must carry them out as far as possible, no matter what the result may be. But what is the final benefit to the public or the shippers of that kind of regulation?

CONFISCATORY RETURNS MUST BE ABOLISHED

Under the Transportation Act of 1920, 5½ per cent, and ½ per cent to be used for improvements, or 6 per cent per annum in all, was established as a fair return for two years on the value of the railroad property as determined by the Interstate Commerce Commission. This year the Interstate Commerce Commission fixed the return at 5¾ per cent. The actual results for the last two years were a return of only 3.47 per cent per annum on such valuation, which we believe is much below their real value. That figure is 40 per cent less than the low return of 5¾ per cent established by the Interstate Commerce Commission, and there is no provision for averaging bad and good years. If over 6 per cent is earned it must be divided with the Government, so that even sound railroads are prevented from using all of their surplus to improve and expand their property, although they may have had many preceding bad years and their credit may demand the retention of all the surplus. I ask you, business men, what expanding business can be founded, or continue successful on a return of 3.47 per cent, or indeed anything less than 6 per cent? Ample transportation service and improvements are impossibilities on any such basis.

This is sad but sure proof that the railroads have no guaranteed income under that Act, and that the Government itself could not finance itself on a 3.47 per cent basis of return. Is it too much to expect that railroad rates should be made without prolonged public argument to earn at least 5¾ per cent per annum?

Here is the entire railroad investment of $20,000,000,000, which, taken as a whole, represents actual value. It is one of the most stable investments in the country. The faith of the citizens and our institutions has continued in that investment. The transportation system of the country is the greatest instrumentality for the success of trade and commerce and the general prosperity of the country. Is it too much to expect that the business men, the farmers and the public generally, who recognize that situation, should appeal to the Interstate Commerce Commission and their own Senators and Representatives, and commercial associations, that rates should be adjusted so as to put beyond any peradventure that at least an average return of 5¾ per cent should be earned on the investment in every year? In a dozen or more years the railroads of the country as a whole only exceeded 5¾ per cent in the year 1916, when 6.1 per cent was earned. If the railroads could be assured of an average return of even 5¾ per cent in good and bad years, the foundation can be laid for railroad credit that will secure sufficient revenue to justify railroad expansion. There can be no such expansion and improvement without the ability to earn a fair return, and have a surplus for emergencies, and to encourage the investors to put additional capital into the business.

The Directors of The Pennsylvania Railroad Company have never wavered in their belief that public opinion is back of a square deal for the railroads, and notwithstanding the discouragement given to railroad investors, we are putting forth every effort to avoid blockades, and under the gravest drawbacks of the last two years we have undertaken the construction of 100 new freight locomotives, 15 new passenger locomotives, 150 passenger coaches, 20 dining cars, and 100 of the latest type cabin cars; and the conversion of a very large number of freight cars from 50-ton to 70-ton capacity. We have actively resumed work with other railroads on the station and yard improvements in Chicago. We are completing our extension into Detroit, enlarging our freight facilities and yards near Harrisburg, South Philadelphia, Pittsburgh, Sharpsburg, and Pitcairn and laying additional tracks from Kenwood to Rochester, Pa., and at other points. We are also proceeding with yard extension at Baltimore and Hagerstown, Md., and other improvements in practically every State in which we are operating. This improvement program is much below what we would like to do if the net earnings had justified it, but there must be a change in the net earnings, or our improvement program must be stopped. We cannot obtain new capital and we must not ask investors to entrust it to us, unless the business men, the farmers, the public and the legislative bodies of the country are going to deal justly with the railroads.

RELIABLE EMPLOYES

Another hope of future progress lies in the loyal and fairly paid body of railroad employes who realize their fair duty to the public and to the railroad owners, and have the good sound sense to do efficient work that will maintain their own position on the payrolls, and their own homes and families. The railroad service is one demanding strict discipline night and day to protect the public and the employes themselves. We all, of course, would like to see an end to railroad strikes. I doubt if it ever will be possible to prevent strikes by any Government edict or order, and I also doubt if it will be possible for any body of men, through strikes or by cutting off the necessaries of life or transportation service, to permanently force the payment out of the pockets of the traveling public of wages that are in excess of the general scale paid in adjacent territory under rather similar conditions. Therefore, no matter how the question is approached, railroad men and railroad management must bow to enlightened and organized public opinion as the ultimate judge. The Pennsylvania Railroad System has most earnestly tried to reproduce a satisfied body of employes, which before the war had the reputation of being among the most polite and intelligent of any railroad employes in the country, and they will prove so again.

Briefly stated, the policy and practice of The Pennsylvania Railroad System in its relation with employes is to give all employes, through their own elected representatives who must also be employes, a voice in the management in all matters affecting their wages, working conditions and welfare, and in other matters of mutual concern affecting the welfare of the company and of the public which the company serves. Membership or non-membership in any union does not concern the management in the practice of the policy on which the officers and the employes have mutually agreed. The primary requisite is that the employes and the management deal directly with each other, and we have tried to avoid outside dictation. It is destructive of good discipline to have cases of individual difference between an employe and a foreman or employing officer, the subject of hearings or orders from an important body like the Labor Board.

Under such mutual co-operation, we can protect the interests of the public, the owners and the employes themselves. Mutual confidence and loyalty are essential to a satisfactory transportation service.

REVISED TAXATION AND LIMITATION OF SUBSIDIZED HIGHWAYS, ETC.

The railroads are already limited under the Transportation Act to a general basis of rates that produce modest returns. Further, individual railroads or systems must divide with the Government if 6 per cent is earned. It seems, therefore, that the railroads being restricted in fixing the price charged for transportation service, and from earning reasonable returns, should have a much more moderate basis of taxation, State and Federal, than at present. The taxes paid by the Pennsylvania Railroad Company in the depressed year of 1921, amounted to over $20,000,000, or thirty cents out of every dollar of its net revenue from railway operations.

Another factor is a change in our taxation policy. The widespread issue of State, Municipal and other securities for unproductive enterprises, and free from taxes, encourages waste that should be checked. It is an injustice to the National Government and is encouraging our people to make investments in tax-free securities, and to make costly and unprofitable improvements, to the neglect of investments in railroads, farming and productive enterprises. Until the country has brought about the deflation of the war costs, and has learned to practise rigorous economies so as to build up a surplus, surely there should be a restriction of capital expenditures and current expenses within the limits of reasonable taxation. There can be little hope of lower living costs and lower taxes, so long as we see large Federal and State outlays, running into hundreds of millions, for non-productive enterprises and for unlimited mileage of new highways, streets, and for some waterways.

State and Municipal obligations have risen from $1,800,000,000 to over $8,000,000,000 in the last twenty years. To this we can add about $23,000,000,000 of National debts, making about $31,000,000,000 in all. Federal, State and Municipal road building and maintenance expenditures for 1919, 1920 and 1921, exceed over one and a half billion dollars. These figures are large enough to justify my suggestion for moderation until war costs are deflated.

These improvements are made practically free to the public for recreational and commercial uses, but the burden of their construction and maintenance is laid on the public, including the solvent productive enterprises of the country, and notably on the railroads. In short, we subsidize roads and waterways, which can take the pick of freight and passenger traffic from the railroads, and which are used for pleasure when the weather is agreeable, and then the authorities throw a large part of the taxes on the railroads to construct and maintain these subsidized commercial and recreational transportation highways. Then complaint is made that railroad rates and charges are too high, and that the railroads will not provide ample and cheap transportation, and their rates should be reduced. Highways and some waterways are essential for recreational and commercial uses; they will become more universally used; but in fairness should not the users pay for their construction and maintenance?

A DEFINITE CONSTRUCTIVE TRANSPORTATION POLICY REQUIRED

If the Municipalities, the States and the Federal Government continue to increase such subsidies, and the railroads are not permitted to charge fair rates so as to pay for wages, materials, taxes, and earn a reasonable return, then the railroads which have proven the cheapest form of transportation must increase their rates very greatly, or all expansion must be impeded, and the weaker railroad lines must be abandoned, or likewise be subsidized by the public authorities. We cannot have an efficient cheap transportation service and continue to play with the railroads and break them down through bad regulation and ruinous taxation. The stronger railroads in the past carried these weak roads, but they can do so no longer, because of their own low returns.

We must not blink at these facts. We must get more sound thinking, prudence in legislation and action, public co-operation, as well as personal initiative to remedy this situation. We must adopt a fair transportation policy. We must build up and not break down. The country cannot continue prosperous unless the railroads, which united it, are prosperous. Railroad prosperity can be assured if railroads are given greater initiative to carry on their work; if they are allowed to earn and pay a fair return to those who are willing to buy and hold railroad bonds and stocks, and if they have a margin of surplus as a credit basis to expand their facilities and equipment, and to protect them against losses, depressions and emergencies.

I thank you very kindly, gentlemen, for your attention.

PRESIDENT SUNNY: I am sure that I express the sentiments of all who are here when I say that we very cordially thank Mr. Rea for coming here this evening, and for his most interesting and enlightening address.

TWO HUNDRED AND EIGHTY-THIRD REGULAR MEETING

The Blackstone

Friday, December 8, 1923

Open Meeting: President B. E. Sunny Presiding
Invocation: Reverend David M. Johnson, S. J.

ADDRESSES:

The Foreign Trade Outlook

Mr. Julius H. Barnes
President United States Chamber of Commerce

American Ships for Foreign Trade
Mr. William H. Stayton
President Baltimore Steamship Company

President Sunny: Ladies, Mr. Barnes, Captain Stayton, fellow members of the Commercial Club and guests: The Merchant Marine is no new subject to this Club. During the past eight years it has been discussed on three different occasions by Homer L. Ferguson, Robert Dollar and the then Secretary of the Treasury, William G. McAdoo.

The following are outstanding paragraphs in two of the addresses, as interesting and timely today. Captain Dollar said:

"What made Great Britain great? It was having ships in every seaport in the world. What would you think of a merchant, having a big store and having to depend on his neighbor across the street for delivery wagons to deliver his goods? That is the exact position we have been in."

Secretary McAdoo said:

"It is folly from an economic point of view to continue deliberately the policy of building up a great foreign trade by leaving to our rivals a control of the vitally important instrumentalities of ocean transportation. So long as our competitors own the ships they make the rates; they control the service and they determine the routes. With this power it is easy to favor their own commerce and discriminate against ours."

A more significant paragraph, with a larger application to the present situation, is taken from Washington's second message to Congress, dated December 8, 1790, exactly 132 years ago today:

"The disturbed situation in Europe, whilst it ought to make us the more thankful for the general peace and security enjoyed by the United States, reminds us at the same time of the circumspection with which it becomes us to preserve these blessings. It requires also that we should not overlook the tendency of a war among the nations most concerned in active commerce with this country to abridge the means, and thereby at least enhance the price, of transporting its valuable products to their proper markets. I recommend it to your serious reflections, how far and in what mode it may be expedient to guard against embarrassments from these contingencies, by such encouragements to our own navigation as will render our commerce and agriculture less dependent on foreign bottoms, which may fail us in the very moments most interesting to both of these great objects."

The Congress, for the reasons stated by President Washington, and, in addition, in recognition of the desperate financial condition of the ship owners and the shipbuilding industry, granted a 10 per cent discount on tariff duties upon imports and exports carried in ships built and owned by American citizens. Subsequently it passed fifty or more tariff and other laws to encourage and protect American shipping, with the result that the traffic increased from 23 to 90 per cent of our exports and imports in the first five years. Of course this increase was very largely at the expense of the ships of Great Britain, and resulted in considerable distress in that country. In 1829 the London Times said:

"The shipping interest, the cradle of our navy, is half ruined. Our commercial monopoly exists no longer, and thousands of our manufacturers are starving or seeking redemption in distant lands. We have closed the Western Indies against America from feelings of commercial rivalry. Its active seamen have already engrossed an important branch of our carrying trade to the Eastern Indies. Her starred flag is now conspicuous on every sea, and will soon defy our thunder."

In 1839 Great Britain adopted its present policy and practice of subsidizing its ships and, due to this and the gradual withdrawal of the beneficial measures previously granted by the Congress, we began steadily to lose tonnage, and in 1853 were carrying less than 70 per cent of our exports and imports. During the Civil War the percentage fell below 30; recovered to 35 in 1870; fell to 17 per cent in 1880; to 11 per cent in 1895, and about the time the World War broke out, it was below 10 per cent.

The Congress of 1790–91 solved the problem of a merchant marine satisfactorily, and we began destroying its work 65 years later and finished the job long ago.

With all of our boasted smartness, in seventy years we have not been able to equal the wise and constructive record of the statesmen of 132 years ago, and our plight with respect to a merchant marine is worse now than ever before.

While of comparatively recent creation, the United States Chamber of Commerce in ten years has made a remarkable record for national helpfulness. With its widespread membership of representative business men; its ingenious and effective methods of communication with every member, it has been quickly able to secure and crystallize the sentiment on public questions for the advice and guidance of the administration and the Congress. As a liaison officer between government and business, its services to both have been invaluable.

Our first speaker is the president of this great organization, and he is in all ways thoroughly well equipped for the exacting responsibility. The largest exporter of grain in the world, he knows the transportation problem in all of its angles and is an ardent advocate of a Merchant Marine.

In the war he performed an extraordinary important service as President of the United States Food Administration Corporation from August, 1917, to July, 1919, and from then to July, 1920, as United States Wheat Director on the appointment of President Wilson. France made him an Officer of the Legion of Honor; and Italy, Belgium, Poland, Finland and Bulgaria also gave him of their most highly prized decorations.

I now have the very great pleasure of presenting to you Julius Howard Barnes, the President of the United States Chamber of Commerce, who will address us on the subject of "The Outlook for Foreign Trade."

THE FOREIGN TRADE OUTLOOK:

ADDRESS BY

MR. JULIUS H. BARNES,
President United States Chamber of Commerce

Mr. Chairman, guests and friends of Chicago: It is a peculiar gratification to appear here as a guest of the Commercial Club. It is well known that your club has performed very effective public service in the past, and every business man knows that there is clearly ahead the need for continned and effective service of those who understand the workings of large economic laws.

The Chamber of Commerce of the United States is especially indebted to Chicago. Of the ten years of its official existence so far traveled, five years have been under the leadership as president of residents of Chicago, and its chief inspirer and its chief inspiration today is a Chicago citizen, a member of your Club.

The Chamber of Commerce of the United States canvassed by a referendum the opinion and conviction of its business membership on the question of the justice and wisdom of Ship Subsidy. The response was unmistakably to the effect that American opinion approved in principle the equalization of the difference in costs between operation in competitive ocean carriage on American standards against the lower standards and lower wage scales of other world carriers. It is clear that business opinion in reaching this conviction seeks to assure two national benefits.

First, that we shall be equipped for ready conversion in time of war with carriers for transport under American ownership and therefore subject to American requisition in time of need. This is a question of national defense on which public opinion may well differ as to degree but hardly as to principle and necessity.

Second, that in the development of new trade routes and in the maintenance of old ones the power of levying rates, both actual and relative, shall not rest in the hands of other nationals whose manufacturing and trading interests may well be served by the indirection of a carrying scale planned for that trade advantage and against American interests.

It is clear that American business opinion demands that steps be taken to establish an American privately owned and privately operated fleet with equality of competition assured it from national revenue, because the service is necessary both in the event of national defense necessity and in the daily, weekly and yearly trade expansion which touches all sections of our people.

Old prejudices and old misconceptions are dislodged only by a long period of convincing logic. It is a curious anomaly that the same sections of our country support the opposition to national grants for equalization of national disability in carriers for our trade expansion and at the same time support the grants of vast sums from national revenues in the guise of adjusted compensation for service which is really beyond all price. The stimulation of foreign trade which would expand employment opportunity at home would benefit far more largely the non-disabled veteran and in a more self-respecting manner. It requires, however, thought and consideration to see this legitimate working of the economic processes and to comprehend that grants of adjusted compensation which spell new and heavier taxation will inevitably tend to stifle enterprise and bring its resultant train of unemployment and distress, which cannot fail to reach every veteran as well.

These are the contradictions of human nature, which, according to our own temperament, provide exasperation or amusement, or furnish the opportunity for insistent educational effort. But whether one believes that national aid in equalization is imperative so that we may have an instrument of conversion to national defense in time of national peril, or whether one believes that the continued expansion of the prosperity of our people depends upon national equalization, one is led naturally into a consideration of the conditions of countries overseas which may justify either the preparation for national defense or the preparation for world trade recovery. One is thus led naturally to study both the political and economic position of Europe because of its dominant position in respect to either of the national necessities for a national merchant fleet. It has three hundred millions of people with their relatively high standard of living and the vast exchange of products and commodities which it impels, providing a most promising outlet for the surplus production of our American farms and industries.

Also in Europe today are centered under governmental direction those international relations which we describe as political in complexion but out of which would grow misunderstandings and rivalries which might lead to international conflict. Therefore, it is well that we examine together the conditions of Europe today, both political and economic, and attempt to measure the trend and possibilities in both relations.

A survey of the Old World conditions today presents, to the superficial observer, many discouraging aspects. It is on these depressing surface observations that we find the basis for current gloomy prophesies, ranging from the milder aspects of famine, despair and hopeless poverty to the ultimate and final entire breakdown of modern civilization.

There is possible, at the same time, a sounder, more searching analysis of the fundamentals of human activity from which can be drawn a more hopeful and more wholesome and a happier expectation for the future of Europe.

A pessimist would make this résumé of Europe, only partly true and largely incomplete:

The Turk, the traditional barbarian and the ruthless despoiler, is back in Europe, against the offended moral sense of the Christian world. Arrogant and defiant, the Turk claims today the right to close, by fortifications, the open seaway of the Dardanelles. Control is thus claimed, by those who have shown no capacity for righteous government, of the only avenue for rescue of the Christian minorities of Armenia and the Caucasus. Control is thus demanded, by those who have shown no capacity for developing trade and commerce, of the only channel between the trade routes of the world and the warm water ports of Russia.

Greece, stripped of its newly acquired expansion, visits with Middle Age savagery upon its luckless servants the result of shameful instances of inefficiency and graft and treachery.

The Balkan States, ancient cradle of world wars, fluctuate between unsound social experiments and tempests of popular passion against discarded ministries threatened with capital punishment for ever daring to assume the responsibilities of state direction.

Russia, its present rulers appearing at the council table of Lausanne with all the pompous braggadocio of the international incompetent, makes its empty boast of armed force with its mythical armies, while its luckless millions of people, in possession of the world's broadest expanse of fertile country, prepare for a new winter of famine, the result of a political and economic system that destroys everything and creates nothing. Embarking deliberately, under fantastic misgovernment, upon a campaign to render worthless all money, the evidence of thrift and effort, it has succeeded in rendering everything within its boundaries worthless, indeed,—even life itself.

Poland, the re-united nation, confirms the historians' doubt as to the self-governing capacity of its people by continned and rapid changes in administration and policies, and by a national scheme of finance which carries no promise of ultimate success.

Austria, content to classify itself under socialist direction as the international mendicant, awaits, almost without hope, the outcome of an experiment of financial and economic administration by more capable peoples, installed at its own request, in utter despair.

Germany, the vast hive of feverish activity, producing much and devouring it all, because also its socialist concept of government embarked the State upon a policy of immoral and dishonest national finance which robs thrift and self-denial of all reward and incentive, deprives industry of the fundamental measure of value on which alone it can healthfully function, destroys its ability to honestly discharge its reparation obligations, and has brought a formerly great and competent people also almost to a state of national beggary.

Italy, boasting since Garibaldi of the possession of a constitution under which the League of Italian States has grown into a great nation, sees the disastrous abdication of government authority two years ago in surrendering private property rights to rebellious factory workmen, followed today by the logical sequence of seizure of power by the Fascisti, without constitutional warrant.

France, enrolling its own man-power in military service, imports three hundred thousand foreign workmen in their stead, and thus burdens its revenues with the cost of possibly excess military organization and loses the productive earnings which imported workmen send outside of France. Blind to the economic lesson of history that no victor can actually collect fifty per cent and more of the entire wealth of a vanquished people, it refuses to face the realities and continues to spend vast sums in excess of its current resources. It offends the moral sense of its traditional friend, America, both by open support of the Turk and by a continued refusal to ratify the naval disarmament treaty, which America looked upon as a first great step in the mutual disarmament of the world.

Great Britain, the greatest of trading nations, dependent for its prosperity on the full employment of its people, faces almost the largest problem of unemployment in its history, today.

These would be the impressions of a pessimist, and in this résumé that type of mind would find the seeds of countless future wars. It is on these superficial aspects that the ominous prophecies of the breakdown of civilization would be based.

But there is a sounder and a more real and hopeful aspect to every one of these particular nations of Europe.

The Turk, at present flushed with intoxication of national victory over his traditional enemy, the Greek, will be held at the Dardanelles by the re-united Christian nations of Europe, until he recovers his sanity and common-sense and until there are assurances given civilization that the barbarous atrocities which have repeatedly stained Turkish misrule shall not be re-enacted.

Greece supplies us with reassurance from its history of a demonstrated passion for democracy, and will resume its normal and proper place in the society of nations, freed from the imperialistic fever which degraded its traditions by the recall of a king who had all but betrayed his country's future during the Great War, and thus jeopardized the former friendship of the world.

The Balkan States have learned the need of economic unity which allows trade and commerce to cross the frontiers of racial hatreds. Mutual agreements facilitating the flow of transportation and the commodities of transport are reducing traditional antagonisms, with stimulated trade and commerce. There is thus provided a sound basis for the future prosperity of their peoples, and this greatly reduces the hazard of unexpected war.

Russia, like a fever patient turning back from death, is able now, by the frightened permission of its fanatic rulers, to partake a little of the diet of national and individual respect for pledges and for private property, which more advanced peoples learned centuries ago. No real recovery is possible until there are re-established constitutional guarantics which protect human life and human activities against the pencil scratch of autocratic edict leveled without notice, and without redress; nor until the security of foreign commerce is assured the individual merchant, and the vain attempt to build overseas trade under a government monopoly, which could destroy an industry over night, is abandoned for the sound and tried processes on which industry can alone provide employment and earnings. Relaxation of edict-destruction, promises of financial and economic reformation, must have a sounder basis of trust than the assertion of those whose whole official record is one of utter repudiation and disregard of human faith. The road is long, for Russia, back to the homely normalities of life, but the inexorable pressure of economic law is starting that country, haltingly, in the right direction.

Poland, in spite of dissension and mistakes, has grasped clearly some of the fundamentals that build the prosperity of a people. It is building its ports and developing steamship service. It is developing its transportation service, until it is one to justify the national pride. It is learning some of those methods which create and maintain the individual prosperity of its people.

Austria still possesses the great capital of a skilled and industrious people, and recently has reached the point of attempting to treat public services of a state with the same honesty of operation to which private individuals must conform. Reducing the unnecessary army of state dependents and raising the charges for public services until they bear some relation to the cost of providing those services, does carry some promise of re-establishing some substitute for the fantastic Austrian crown which will facilitate the industry and commerce of its people, now functioning clumsily on the cumbersome methods of ancient trade and barter.

Germany, through the wreck and despair of its formerly thrifty people, at least has so discredited the experiment and tenets of socialism that, today, the socialist party refuses the responsibilities of the present government. As always, in time of crises, the business man of Germany has been obliged to volunteer, applying the common-sense and experience of his calling, to try and prevent the final wreck brought on by social experiments which have always failed under actual test in the past. It is still true that, in Germany, the thoughtless and the reckless make and spend in spectacular dissipation; the poor and the decent suffer in silence the evils of their present economic system, but it is also true that there is an increasingly clear acceptance of the responsibility for the destruction of a disastrous war, and a purpose to repair, as far as the national capacity may allow. A settlement of the reparations question within the practical limits of the honest attempt of the German people to perform, and with the assurance of ultimate redemption which that implies, would make effective the needed financial aid to France and Belgium and would start the processes of industry in Central Europe.

Italy has demonstrated that at least its new rulers have an extraordinary honesty of purpose in public service, and a tenacity of will that promises to make for sound national progress.

France still possesses the capital of the world admiration for its dauntless courage and unrivaled endurance. If it seems today to tend towards dreams of militarism, based on the new sense of power which its present republican empire of one hundred million people might inspire, yet we may be sure that the day will come soon with its old true perspective of its proper place. The friendship of the world and its own hard sense will find some assurance for its national security against attack other than the present one of unbearable military burdens. Some just and fair way will be devised to secure from Germany the restitution to which France is entitled and within the limits of Germany's efforts in good faith to pay. Relieved of its traditional fear of unprovoked attack and with the unrivaled willingness of its people at home to work and to save, France will vindicate the confidence and trust of those who know it best and love it most.

Great Britain, taxing its people at a rate which can be laid indeed on few peoples without rebellion, is working its way slowly back to its former dominant position in world trade and world finance. A measure of its recovery is the steady march to gold parity of the pound sterling, which has now reached the highest point of recovery since the armistice.

And then we have Czechoslovakia, displaying a vision in the economics of government and industry, and a fidelity in materializing that vision, which is establishing that country on the securest of foundations.

Then there are the Baltic States, split off from the great mother country of Russia, fortunately influenced in their social, political and economic policy by their closer contact with the saner outside world. Their order and progress is in marked contrast to the disorganization of their former mistress. This is evidenced, for instance, by the estimate the world of commerce places upon the ruble of Latvia, which, with something of honest purpose behind it, sells at 250 to the dollar, while the Russian ruble itself is at the fantastic nothingness of ten to fifteen million to the dollar.

Summarizing Europe as a whole, the fever of war is well out of the blood of its peoples. There is clear indication of the almost universal desire to work and to produce, no matter how small the present promise. Those countries that have developed sound financial policies and honest practices, like any thrifty individual, are working their way back to normal and healthy processes of life. Their progress is shown by the gold parity of their currencies, spelling the ability to trade overseas, to exchange commodities, to supply the wants of their own people, and to sell the prodncts of their own industries. Switzerland, Holland, Sweden and Japan, together with Canada and the United States, are islands of honest administrative functioning which are recording their currency denominations on the parity of gold. Spain and Great Britain lack but five to seven per cent of full recovery. When Great Britain, the financial mistress of the world, attains the nominal gold parity, then there will be resumed the liquid flow of gold in settlement of trade balances, the breaking down of trade barriers, and the elimination of trade hazards, and the wheels of the world's industry will revolve with new activities.

Those who forecast the economic collapse of Europe—nay, more, even those who doubt its steady progress toward certain and actual recovery, fail to grasp the fundamentals on which human activities are sustained.

The figures of coal output, of railroad transport, of steel output, of textile operation, the great indices which measure the opportunities for employment of a people, all today trend in the right direction. The marvellous recovery in America from the partial suspension of industry a year ago, recorded then in the army of four million of unemployed, to today's substantial prosperity and activity, is the forerunner of a probably similar, though less spectacular, recovery in Europe; but first Europe must establish honesty in national administration, as in individual relations; and establish political systems which revolve around that ideal of honest responsibility to their people, before the processes of industry can be quickened into full production.

How can these people of Europe fail to realize, out of their past and present suffering, that the recovery of national prosperity and the recovery of individual content and comfort, depends primarily on the aggregate effort of every one of its individual citizens? How can they fail to realize that that individual effort can be inspired and stimulated only by a system of government which assures to every individual the rewards fairly apportioned by society through the processes of trade, as the only fair expression of the value of service, through invention, by manufacture or production, by distribution or by any other service in the social structure? How can they fail to realize that this fair reward, so apportioned by fair and open competition, not bestowed and not denied in the human judgment of any ruler or set of rulers, must also be secured to the earner, and to the dependents whose affection inspire his effort? How can they fail to realize that, out of the aggregate individual efforts thus stimulated and protected, will come the total production which builds both individual and national prosperity?

The contrast today, between the substantial prosperity of America, holding high its living standards, and the deprivation and despair of Europe, is due to something more fundamental than fortunate geographical position or superior natural resources. The explanation lies in the inspiration to individual effort and accomplishment inherent in the American tradition of government. The whole record of our relatively short national history confirms the wisdom of the social and political philosophy in which this republic was founded, the theory that government exists primarily for the preservation of equal opportunity for the maintenance of fair play between individuals and that sound national progress, as also individual prosperity, rests upon the incentive to individual effort. The conception that each individual should carve his own niche in the social structure by his own character, ability, and effort, has been the moving force that has built this new Republic into the world leadership of social and living standards. It has prevented the establishment in America of the deadly caste system, which stifles ability and retards social progress. The directors of industry today are largely men who served their apprenticeship in the ranks of workers and employees. There is a constant ferment in the social mass because

America's individualism holds assurance of security in the enjoyment of certain reward for exceptional service.

Organized business realizes more keenly than other sections of our people how easily unwise relation of government to industry may stifle the spirit of enterprise and the will to create and produce, with its resultant individual distress and disaster. On organized business, therefore, rests a peculiar responsibility of leadership in the preservation of the field of individual opportunity in which alone the hopes and convictions and aspirations of millions of our coming young people can be realized.

The relation of government to industry can be effected in the preservation of this precious heritage by leadership which is patient, but persistent, equipped with convincing logic and inspired by this great ideal.

In the last few years, the Chamber of Commerce of the United States has had occasion on several major national questions to speak the voice of the organized business of America. In no respect has its voice or its action violated the fundamentals of this philosophy of fair play. Organized business has seen the establishment in Washington of agencies pleading for and laboring to secure the special interest of special sections of our people. The necessarily narrow aims of these special agencies gave them a peculiar effectiveness in directing influence and pressure. Only within the last ten years and through the Chamber of Commerce of the United States, has organized business been able to speak with the force and authority of national conviction behind it. Moreover, the very multiplicity of activities comprised within organized business would greatly embarrass its work if it attempted to act for single interest of any single section or any single industry. Therefore it has found its justification and its security in applying to every act of national leadership the underlying principle of national fair play.

It was in this spirit that it helped to secure the establishment of a Federal Reserve Banking Act which demonstrated its soundness and effectiveness in the great strain of an unexpected war.

It helped to establish a national budget by which the Nation's receipts and expenditures are estimated and compared, leading to care and study and economy in national administration.

It helped to secure a revision of unwise taxation laws which were stifling the spirit of enterprise, until a year ago the result was written in the national record of 4,000,000 unemployed.

It helped to further the adoption of a discretionary clause in the application of duties in the last tariff law by which some measure of flexibility is possible to meet the ever-changing conditions of overseas trade.

It helped to cultivate a national sentiment in this country which recognized if America is to have an American fleet in competition with the fleets of the world, and ready for conversion to national defense in event of war, it must, through some form of subsidy, equalize the excessive operating costs occasioned largely by our own navigation law requirements.

It helped to secure a revision of the railroad laws by which there is restored some measure of fair treatment to the railroads and opened to them some opportunity for possible earnings, by care and skill, as will maintain and develop these railroads with the ever-increasing tonnage of the country.

It helped to secure and make effective generous expenditures from our national treasury to aid those who suffered disability in national service in our defense, and it opposed granting gigantic sums to those uninjured without providing the revenues from which those gigantic sums, largely unasked and unnecessary, should be paid. This would easily have been the first step upon the dangerous road of inflation which has led to utter ruin in so many countries of Europe.

The Chamber of Commerce of the United States has an abiding faith in the effectiveness of government by a free people intelligently informed and with an honesty of purpose expressed in this philosophy of fair play.

It believes the army of unemployed was eliminated by the resourcefulness and enterprise of individuals and communities, informed of the situation, and willing to assume the commercial hazards of reviving suspended industries and to establish new industries; aided also, fortunately, at the same time, by fairer taxation that left some inducement to commercial ventures.

It has just assisted in solving the problem of coal distribution by the co-operative effort of industry and individuals rather than by the processes of law and regulation. The coal situation has been solved, broadly speaking, and the menace which followed five months' partial suspension of production has been rendered harmless, and by voluntary action. Accurate information to the public, and an appeal to self-restraint by industries in buying, quickened the normal processes of supply and demand and made effective to the utmost the current production. In that, there has been a great national object lesson written in confirmation of the effectiveness of voluntary co-operation in industry.

If there had been no national business leadership and no national contact with industry and organized business in this country, this great demonstration of national team-play could not have been made so instantly effective.

I leave to you to place your own value on the demonstration that there are more effective means at hand for the correction of large-scale social and industrial evils and defects, than the multiplying of legislation upon legislation and regulation upon regulation, invading every man's business and every man's home.

The Chamber is today erecting in Washington a national home for American business, the gift of the business men of the United States, costing two and one-half millions of dollars, to symbolize the dignity and stability of American enterprise. In efficiency of service, in material aid to all the processes of trade and industry, it will fulfill the expectation of its friends and will satisfy the American passion for effective accomplishment. But if it is to speak the voice of American business, if it is to present the rightful aims of American commerce and industry to which its leadership entitles it, it can do so only with the continued and loyal support of every organization in America such as your own.

The men who administer the national chamber have a sober sense of their responsibility and a solemn appreciation of the trust reposed in them by this position of leadership. They realize that every American home reflects the stimulated hopes and ambitions secured by a social and political philosophy made effective in daily life through the processes of trade and industry when demonstrated in the American conception of equality, of opportunity and of individual fair play.

President Sunny: The full force of the unsatisfactory condition of our Merchant Marine falls on the ship owner and operator. The rest of us are affected less directly.

The testimony of the next speaker is based on many years of intimate relations with maritime affairs at home and abroad.

Captain Stayton graduated from Annapolis in 1881 and was Second Lieutenant in the United States Marine Corps for many years. He was then Judge Advocate in New York, and during the Spanish-American War was a captain in charge of a large fleet of gunboats.

For some twenty years he has been engaged in the steamship business in the foreign trade, and is the President of the Baltimore Steamship Company. He is a member of the Executive Committee of the National Merchant Marine Association.

He has been a persistent and industrious campaigner for the United States Merchant Marine for a great many years, and many of you may have had the pleasure of hearing him on one or the other of the two occasions when he spoke to large audiences in Chicago four years ago.

I now have the pleasure of presenting Captain William H. Stayton, who will speak to you on the subject of "American Ships for Foreign Trade."

AMERICAN SHIPS FOR FOREIGN TRADE:

ADDRESS BY

MR. WILLIAM H. STAYTON,

President Baltimore Steamship Company

Mr. President, ladies and gentlemen: Perhaps I will get my foundation best if I give a little résumé of our progress in merchant marine, as I see it.

About one hundred years ago we were practically foremost in the fight for ocean carrying trade. At about that time we began to slide. We gradually went down for nearly a century. In 1917, when we went into the war, we did not have vessels enough to transport our own troops overseas. The measure of what we accomplished is shown by the fact that we had twenty-eight battleships, which you had paid for, you taxpayers, and because we did not have auxiliaries to send them abroad we hid them in Yorktown harbor. Before the armistice came we succeeded in getting five out of the twenty-eight to the other side, and we never did get but five of our battleships in the war zone, all for lack of a merchant marine.

We began then to pay in 1917 the penalty for national neglect. You had to build a fleet utterly regardless of economy and cost. You spent very nearly in fleet and appurtenances four billion dollars, and when the armistice came you had that fleet on your hands. It was managed for about two years under Government control before you took stock. Before stock was completely taken you were losing about two hundred million dollars a year in operation. Then you had stock taken. You passed the law of 1920, which was the first law in which America had ever laid down a policy. She is departing just as rapidly from it now as she can, apparently. The language of the preamble of the law, the first part of it, is worth reading.

Resolved by Congress: "that it is necessary for the national defense and for the proper growth of its commerce that the United States shall have a merchant marine sufficient to carry the greatest portion of its commerce, and serve as an able auxiliary in time of emergency, . . . to be owned and operated privately by citizens of the United States.

"And it is hereby declared to be the policy of the United States to do whatever may be necessary to develop and encourage the maintenance of such a merchant marine, . . . and officers and others must keep always in view this purpose and object as the primary end to be obtained."

That was two years ago. That law provided for the appointment of a board, which should determine what should be done in order that we might have a merchant marine. A board of seven commissioners was appointed, each one having the pay of a cabinet officer. There were some Democrats, some Republicans, some appointed by Mr. Wilson, some by Mr. Harding—and I have never heard their competency questioned. They employed experts, some of them getting three times as much pay as any cabinet officer. Their competency is quite beyond question in the shipping world.

The board and those experts, as ordered by this law,

devised a plan which they thought would solve the difficulty. They submitted it to the President of the United States, who, after some changes, approved it. There was then held a joint conference of the United States Senate Committee on Commerce and the House Committee on Merchant Marine. Six months were spent in taking testimony, and then a majority of both the House and Senate Committees approved the measure that is now pending before the Congress, known as the Ship Subsidy Bill. Congress is now considering it, and the members of Congress are going to decide in just what form it shall pass.

There is, it seems to me, a great deal of misinformation concerning what that law proposes. It is frequently said that the law contemplates the expenditure of a hundred million dollars a year for an indefinite number of years; this money to be taken out of the pockets of the taxpayers and used to enrich a few steamship owners on the eastern seaboard. As a matter of fact, not one cent is to be taken out of the pockets of the taxpayers, but, instead, money put in. The total expenditures will average twenty-two million dollars a year for ten years. Very little, if any, of the money will remain with the ship owners, and none of it ought to.

It seems to me that you in Chicago, in addition to your interest as American citizens in this matter, have two special interests. First, it is easy to compute just how much of the money from this city, the money you invested in Liberty Bonds, went into the building of this fleet. The actual figures show that you spent one hundred and fifty-five million dollars of your money in Chicago for the building of this fleet, and that fleet you still own, you taxpayers. Because it is over the hills, you do not see the fleet. You do not seem to realize how vital your interest in it is. But if you would for a moment realize it is like a factory, a part of your city, having cost you one hundred and fifty-five million dollars and having been built by you as a war aid to the Government and if you would go out and look at it, you would decide whether you wanted to junk it or scrap it or keep it running for the benefit of your country and city.

You are just as much interested in this fleet, even though it is over the hills. It is yours.

There is a second reason why you should be alert about this matter. It is because that fleet has been built and operated under the direction of people from your city. Mr. Hurley, Mr. Piez, Mr. Heyworth and Mr. Carry were the heads of the departments that founded the fleet and made it possible. Judge Payne and Mr. Lasker from your City of Chicago have been the men who operated it since the war. I do not believe there was ever a more worthy set of men that got together; I do not believe any set of men in the world undertook a greater task and I do not believe any set of men in the world ever completed such a task with less mistakes and less scandals.

Of course, they made mistakes. Who could undertake such a task as that and not make mistakes? If I had made no more mistakes in my life than those men made in the development of that fleet, I would today be sailing a wet yacht under a foreign flag and not going around making speeches for the American merchant marine.

That is the situation today. This law is pending and you are, it seems to me, vitally interested in it. I am going to ask myself, as I go along, a few questions and try to answer them. I shall be unable to touch all of the important points, but what I do say will, I hope, give you some idea of what this means.

It seems to me a good question to ask ourselves in the first instance how much is the United States interested in a foreign trade. One of your Illinois men, Professor Zimmerman, down at Decatur, the James Millikin University, has recently computed that the goods exported from the United States in a normal year, if loaded in freight cars, of about 25 tons to the car, would make annually a train 24,000 miles long.

Any man who will stop to realize that carloads of goods 24,000 miles long go out of the United States every year and what would happen if they were dumped back on the home market and how prices would tumble and how men would be kept out of employment and how bankruptcy and panic would follow, would know how we are interested in foreign trade better than I can tell him.

The next question, it seems to me, is how much is the far West interested in foreign trade. Seventy per cent of all goods exported is from the Mississippi Valley. Two-thirds of the advantage of foreign trade is yours. And if disaster follows, two-thirds of it will come to you. That is to say, the interest of the Mississippi Valley in foreign trade is twice as great as all other sections of the country put together. It is nonsense to talk about a merchant marine and foreign trade having only to do with the sea coast.

I suppose the next question to be asked is, can we have a proper foreign trade without a merchant marine under the American flag, or must we carry our trade under the American flag? Perhaps it would be better, it seems to me now, to ask that question the other way, and put it: Why should we not carry it under the American flag?

We have the ships. Why not do it? But let us assume for a moment we have no ships. I should say then it would be wise to go ahead and build the ships to carry our trade. If you stop to think the matter over a little bit you realize that you cannot have a proper trade unless you do carry your own goods. Of course, we have been prosperous in some respects, even when the foreigners carried our goods for us. But every man knows he has made mistakes which have kept him from becoming 100 per cent prosperous. The United States has made a great mistake in not having its own fleet, thereby not being able to enjoy that 100 per cent success.

Mr. Barnes touched on a vital question, that of regulating rates, that you cannot regulate rates when the ships are foreign. You have been alert in this part of the country to regulate the railroads and to see that all that went to the seaboard was carried under proper rates, non-discriminatory, that the practice of rebating was stopped and that you were given fair and equal rates. Yet when you got as far as the seacoast you closed your eyes and forgot to look twice as far beyond that, to the fact that the foreigner was going to carry these goods, carry them twice as far as they had been transported in this country, when you knew that his laws permitted him to have rebates, and perquisites of like nature; you knew he was allowed to favor his nationals. If you, of this part of the country, have established anything definite as a lesson to the world, it is the principle that transportation belongs to the people as a whole, and not to the man who happens to own the means of transportation. But you visualized that only as far as the seacoast. It would be just as ridiculous as if you regulated the carriage of your goods as far as Newark, New Jersey, but that on the remaining five miles you would let the railroads charge all they pleased and do all they pleased without interference from you.

There are many other reasons as to why you should not let other ships carry your own goods. It seems almost unnecessary to go into them. You know the thing that causes war in the world is commercial rivalry. You know other nationals want this very trade that you have. You cannot expect them to carry your goods and hold the trade for you. They would carry one class of your goods, your grain and the things they want to eat, yes, but when it came to those things in which they are your rivals they do not give you the same service.

For instance, one time, I was down at the town of Santos, and saw 120 packages unloaded from one ship, 117 from a foreign country, the other 3 packages containing American goods, Thermos bottles, sewing machines and typewriters. The 117 foreign packages landed safely. The 3 American packages were permitted to slip out of the slings from the boom end and smash 25 feet on the granite dock below.

I afterwards went to see the man who was to receive the Thermos bottles. He had a letter from the captain, who said when the bottles came aboard they were all broken, that "the lying, swindling American manufacturer is trying to make you pay for broken glass."

When I got back to New York I went to see the American Thermos bottle manufacturer. He also had a letter from that same captain, who said, "the lying, swindling Brazilian is trying to avoid paying for these goods. They were in perfect condition. I know that, because I saw them."

It so happened that the vice-president of the steamship line on which I was traveling was also one of the owners of a large Thermos bottle plant in Europe, and they wanted the trade in Thermos bottles, and they have it.

If the other man is manufacturing something in Europe that he wants to sell in competition with you, it is a pretty sure assumption that he will not carry or handle your goods as carefully as he will his own.

I remember our ancestors used to have a saying, which was: If you really want to raise your child, don't turn it over to a hostile Indian to be brought up. If you want your foreign trade, don't turn it over to your enemy to be brought up. In other words, you cannot have the proper foreign trade unless you have vessels, under your control, so that you may regulate the rates and regulate the practices under which that trade is handled.

You hear often that Americans do not know how to pack goods for export, that the goods they send abroad are smashed in transit, while the goods of the foreigner are packed so they are not smashed in transit. There may be some little truth in that, but I would first advise you to look up and see whether those goods went on a foreign ship or not. You will then very frequently see the reason why there was the smashing.

The next question, it seems to me, that I ought to ask, is: Assuming that we must have a merchant marine under our flag to handle our goods, can we do so without some sort of government encouragement, aid, regulation, subsidy, or whatever you may be pleased to call it? Can we have a merchant marine of our own without government stabilization?

Just apply it to your own business. It makes no difference what the business is. Let me cite the case of the banker. Ask your own selves. Apply it to your own business. Suppose you were engaged in the business of banking, and, having established a prosperous business, a foreigner comes in and settles alongside of you. He is not required to live up to our banking laws; not required to keep any reserves, nor make any reports to the state officers. In addition he is allowed to bring his own people in and pay them foreign wages; and not only that, but is permitted to bring in all the clothing they wear and their household furniture and food without payment of any duty at the custom house.

Let us suppose that foreign government desires to get that business in its own people's hands and pays that man several thousand dollars a year in order that he may live and run you out of business. Just how soon would your employes begin to complain about that state of affairs and just how soon would you yourself be ready to say that your government ought to help you out and not permit foreigners to come in and run you out of business? In short, could you run your business under those circumstances without some sort of aid from the government?

I have not the least doubt that that is what is happening in the shipping industry now. The vessels of the foreigner come to your port; they pay no duties; they pay the foreign wage to their people; they get the bonus subsidies from their nations, and they are putting your ships out of business, just as they would put your banks out of business if you would let them come in here and do that. It is just as unfair to subject us to that treatment as it would be to subject you to it in your own business.

Another answer to that question as to whether we can run without some sort of stabilization from the government is that other nations do not do it. Take the case of the International Merchant Marine Company, ninety per cent owned by Americans, but so stifled by the regulations that we would not let them live under our flag; yet American money bought the fleet, but when the war broke out Great Britain took those ships and used them during the war, and you had to spend four billion dollars to build the fleet you wanted, simply because you had forced and driven that fleet into the hands of Great Britain.

It seems ridiculous that we Americans are doing that kind of thing. It is not possible we know more about it than the nationals of the other parts of the world who have run these fleets. It is not possible that we know more about it than Great Britain. Instead of trying to do as we have, perhaps we ought to adopt some of her methods which have been so highly successful. For these reasons I think you cannot have a merchant fleet without some kind of government stabilization.

The next question is: How much does it cost? Perhaps the first thing is, Who pays, how much, and who gets the money?

The present bill contemplates a subsidy, starting at about $14,000,000 and ending at $30,000,000, an average of $22,000,000 for ten years. But that money, that $220,000,000 subsidy, does not come out of your pockets. Here is the situation:

Today you own this fleet and it is idle. It is costing you $50,000,000 a year to keep it in idleness, and if you hold it for ten years it will be worthless. During those ten years you will lose the interest, depreciation, and you will lose $50,000,000 a year. Sell it. Somebody is going to buy it for, let me say, a billion dollars. That is the approximate value of it today. But whatever the price,—call it $500,000,000, if you want—somebody is going to buy it, or a number of people are going to buy it, for $500,000,000. They are going to pay the interest on the deferred payments, and are going to stop this $50,000,000 a year loss you are having. Out of that $500,000,000 that they are paying into your treasury you are going to pay them back—out of their own money, mind you—a refund, to encourage them, to keep them going, until they get on their feet. Not one cent of it comes from the taxpayers, but, on the other hand, out of the purchase price which they pay you, you will have paid them back their $220,000,000 and you will have a good many hundreds of million dollars left in the treasury. It is unfair to say they are going to come and tax you in order to support the fleet.

Of course, you may say that we can sell the fleet, without that. Well, we have been trying for about four years and have spent a hundred million dollars, and have a fleet that, by reason of deterioration, is worth 20 per cent less than it was six years ago, and in the meantime you have gone along with all the loss of interest and have had to carry the insurance risk.

I do not believe you can handle this proposition without governmental aid, and if you do give the aid, as I say, the men who buy the ships pay you your money back. Our people ought to know from where the money is coming, from those who buy the fleet.

We might also ask ourselves what it will cost us if we do not do this. Your fleet will go to junk. You will watch it while you pay $50,000,000 a year for letting it dwindle to worthlessness, and then you have to sell it for junk; it will be a dead loss.

Further than that, you will again face the possibility of war, and when war comes you will again have to pay four billion dollars to build a fleet, while if you do encourage the people who are trying to buy the fleet you will have that fleet available, which you can commandeer in time of war, and you will not have to build one.

In short, I believe the man who asks himself the question: "How much will it cost if we do it, and how much will it cost if we don't do it?" will realize its cheapness to do it.

After all, the best answer is that the dollar mark is not the only standard by which you can judge a merchant fleet. We have the four-power treaty, as you know. We have said that we are going to keep a fleet equal to the biggest. Are we keeping our plighted word if we keep our battleships up and let our merchant marine go to ruin, and then find ourselves in the same condition we did in 1917, when we were unable to get the battleships out of Yorktown harbor? We must keep our merchant marine if we are going to keep our word in the four-power treaty, even if it does cost money. The dollar mark is not the sole standard of a man's honor.

Take the ordinary sales department of a manufacturing concern. It does not produce. It costs money. That is no reason for doing away with it. When somebody tells me the merchant marine is going to cost us money and seems to think that that is the end of the argument, he does not know what he is talking about. This Club costs money. It is not productive. But you would not destroy it. Your chambers of commerce all cost money, and they perform the same functions as a merchant marine. Your merchant marine goes abroad and sells your goods, but if the men who man the ships, the officers, are not Americans, your goods will not be sold.

Another question we might ask ourselves is: Is there any history behind this, any history to guide us? Mr. Sunny told you of that first law. It always seemed to me a rather fine thing that when our forefathers, after the adoption of the Constitution, met in the first Congress, they passed law No. 1, which will always remain law No. 1 of the United States, that that law was a law with exactly the same title as this bill has down in Washington today, a law to encourage and develop the American merchant marine. That bill which was then drawn was framed by a committee which included among its members Adams and Hamilton of the North, and Jefferson and Madison of the South, and it was signed by George Washington. It started when we were only carrying 23 per cent of our foreign trade in our own bottoms, and within five years we were carrying 90 per cent, and we continued to carry 90 per cent as long as that law remained on the books, and it remained there so long that people forgot who had passed it, what it was about, and not realizing that that was the law that had made our merchant marine. It was analogous to the old biblical saying: "There arose a generation which knew not Joseph." So they repealed that law and gradually we sunk back to the condition in which we found ourselves in 1917.

There is much in that law for us to learn. Men who ask whether we have history behind us may well study that law and find that our forefathers built it wisely.

The present bill contemplates two forms of aid, a direct aid, which is a money payment, and an indirect aid, which does not cost the taxpayers anything, but gives business to the ships. For example, it requires that fifty per cent of the immigrants coming to this country shall come under the American flag. That costs you taxpayers no money, but it does bring business to the American ships. There are many other examples of indirect aid.

But it is true that some direct aid must be given, because your law as at present is unfair. Let me take the matter of prohibition. That is the last thing that has come up. I do not believe personally that liquor should be sold aboard American ships. I am in accord with the Attorney General's ruling in that matter. You have that ruling that liquor must not be sold on American ships, and the American public, that made the law which says that liquor must not be sold on American ships, when the time comes for them to go traveling to Europe, say, "We will not travel on your rotten old ships, because they are not up to date." That is not fair.

There are many little things of that sort which the American people do by their laws. Within the last two months a steamboat inspector came to me and told me that I had to put on one of my ships three additional water tenders. I said, "There is no use of it." He said, "I know that." I asked, "What is the trouble?" He replied, "Mr. Stayton, I will lose my job unless the labor unions back me up, and they told me I would have to do it, that is why I do this." I said, "It will cost me $375 a month." "I am sorry, but you will have to do it." I said, "You know there is a Jap vessel running against me?" "Yes." "In exactly the same trade?" "Yes." "Trying to beat me out on that trade?" "Yes." "Are you going to insist that I put on these water tenders?" "Yes, I cannot do anything but insist on it."

Therefore, I am paying out $375 a month. But I do say to you that if you penalize me because I happen to be an American and not a Jap, you ought to pay for it. There ought to be an appropriation to look out for that sort of injustice.

The commission, which is far abler than I am, has studied this matter for two years. They have decided to give as much indirect aid as they can and to give direct pay for such injustices as I have cited, that inflict these things on the American ship owners who keep within the law. Then they say, in ten years you can repeal your law and put the American ship owner on an equality with the foreign ship owner, and after that no additional direct aid will be necessary.

The next question I want to ask is: What is the objection? What objection is there to it? The principal objection, I believe, comes from the foreigner. I do not mean to say that he is unfair. I do not mean to accuse him. If you will place yourself in the position where you have a hauling contract which paid from three hundred million dollars to five hundred million dollars every year gross—which our ocean freight does pay the foreigner—if you had a contract of that nature which paid you gross three hundred million dollars to five hundred million dollars, and the man for whom you were doing the hauling began to discuss the question of whether he would build his own trucks and do his own hauling, you would go and tell him that he ought not to do it; you would tell him that he would do this, that and the other thing, disastrous to him, run over children in the streets; and you would endeavor to keep him out of the business. The foreigner is trying to do just that thing to us.

There is opposition in the Middle West, unhappily, I think; opposition based on lack of information concerning it. It is so far from the seashore that people from the Middle West sometimes do not understand, just as the people on the Eastern Seaboard do not quite understand why the farmer wants some sort of special aid. But the answer, I think, to that sort of thing is not to say, "Oh, that is subsidy; we won't give it." Because, after all, the farmer of the states west is asking for some kind of subsidy. Our agricultural department is practically a subsidy in favor of the farmer. A great many things are being done today in the nature of subsidy. The building of roads is an outstanding example. You are going to have some day a route from Chicago through the St. Lawrence to the ocean. When that comes you will have to have a subsidy. The best thing is to give and take. Say to the East, "You can have the subsidy on ships, and when our time comes, we want your assistance in giving us the things we need."

That brings me to the next question: What can we here do? This evening would be a waste of time if I did not suggest something specific. It seems to me you can do this: This bill is going to come up in the Senate in a short time and then come before the House. I take it the most of you know your Congressmen and Senators. Their sentiment is not favorable, throughout the Middle West. Practically all the Iowa delegation is against the bill. Yet Iowa has a hundred million dollars' interest in the bill, having spent that for the building of ships, and does not know it. You have friends throughout the West. If you believe in this sort of thing, won't you drop a letter to some of your friends, in other states and other congressional districts and ask them to write to their representatives and say: "We think it possible that the Central West has a vital interest in this matter; we hope that you, as members of Congress, will look into the matter and see whether it is worth while." A few more letters from this section of the country will pass the bill.

I wish some of you would invest in steamships. Most of us do make some money, because we base a large part of our traffic on the coastal trade or on the run to Porto Rico or the Philippines, where foreigners are not permitted to compete. We use that as the backbone or foundation and build up the foreign service on that. Our vessels are not losing money. I make this suggestion in the hope that you will come to know more about the steamship business, steamship rates and steamship trade. It would not be difficult for you as a group to pick out some steamship corporation that is paying dividends and wisely run and invest a few thousand dollars in it and put one of your group on the board of directors, so that you might study the situation and have brought home to you what it means. My experience is that the man who goes into the steamship business has more opportunities for developing his trade and picking up new business than anything else I know of can give him. That is the thing that I do wish you would look over.

Some of the newspapers out here criticize the bill. I saw one criticism the other day which seemed to me to be as fair a criticism as I had seen. It said in substance that we will go ahead and give the subsidy and then Great Britain will give a larger subsidy, and we will give a larger subsidy, and so on; that it is a matter of accumulation, and in the end we will have bankruptcy.

Not at all. It seems to me to be a situation that tests the very fiber of Americanism. We invented the game of poker and know something about bluff. The nations of the world are bluffing us today. Are we going to lay down our cards when we have the winning hand? They are telling us what we can do, and we are almost ready to quit. Whereas, if we stood pat and did nothing more than say, "We own these ships; we are not going to permit them to be sold; we are going to own and operate our own merchant marine," the same thing will happen as happened in the four-power treaty. They will say, "We cannot very well match you in the building of ships, if your government is behind you, no more than we could match you in the building of battleships. Let us talk it over. How much do you want to carry?" And we will answer, in the terms of the law of 1920, "We only want to carry one-half of our trade," which is fair. They will agree to it; the business will be divided half and half, and the whole proposition of subsidies throughout the world will stop. The world will be better. Don't let them bluff us out of the perfectly secure position in which we stand today.

Now for our last point, stop and look at what the price is.

After every great war what does the world do or what do the devastated nations do? They turn to some new land where they can wrest riches from the soil, where they can reimburse themselves for the wealth that is destroyed.

After the Civil War the North and South, both impoverished, turned toward the West. There they found the mines and agriculture and the forests. They had to build transportation. But your forefathers developed in this western country something that not only made the North and South as rich as they were before, but made this country incalculably richer than it had ever been.

Now almost the whole world is impoverished. It has got to turn somewhere. It must turn to one of two places, South America or the Far East. To my mind it will be China and eastern Siberia; for there are the riches and also the labor. All they need is transportation. But whether the world turns to South America or to the Far East, if you have not the ships you are not going to share in that development. If your forefathers had said, "No grants or subsidies to the railroads; we will not permit these railroads to run to the West, from the East to the western country, because we won't help you," then the western country would not have been developed as it has been and the great riches that have come out of the West, and have made Chicago, would not have been yours; and if we today of America stand in the way of that connecting link that is going to tie us up with this new development that is about to come within the next twenty-five years, if you in the West stand in the way of our getting those ships, you will have deprived the coming generation of that wonderful opportunity which you have enjoyed out here. I believe you owe it to your children to write those letters to the Senators and Congressmen and to write your friends to get them to help you out.

MR. JAMES O. HEYWORTH: Mr. President, on behalf of

the members of the Commercial Club I wish to extend both to Mr. Barnes and Captain Stayton our friendship and also express our appreciation of their coming here and addressing us as they have. I wish it were possible here tonight for this meeting, 100 per cent, to express themselves in favor of restoring once again the supremacy of the merchant marine of this country on the seas of the world.

MR. SUNNY: Mr. Heyworth has truly spoken for all of us in his thanks to the speakers of the evening. We have been greatly entertained and enlightened through their efforts. The meeting is now adjourned.

TWO HUNDRED AND EIGHTY-FOURTH REGULAR MEETING

THE BLACKSTONE
SATURDAY, JANUARY 13, 1923.

Open Meeting: President B. E. Sunny Presiding
Invocation: The Right Reverend Charles P. Anderson, D.D.

ADDRESS:

LABOR, IMMIGRATION AND CITIZENSHIP
HONORABLE JAMES J. DAVIS.

PRESIDENT SUNNY: Mr. Secretary, guests and fellow members: This is the initial appearance of two young men whom we have just elected to membership in this Club, and I want to extend to them a very cordial and a very sincere welcome. I refer to Mr. James A. Patten—will Mr. Patten please stand up?—and Brigadier General Abel Davis,—will General Davis please arise? (Mr. Patten and General Davis were received with vigorous applause.)

In dealing with the fundamental questions of "Labor, Immigration and Citizenship," our distinguished speaker will not be biased in his judgment by doctrines or theories absorbed in the schoolhouse, because he left it when he was eleven years of age. What he will say will come from the larger and sounder school of actual experience, in which he has been a close and industrious student for some forty years, not merely as an observer or investigator, but as a laborer; as an immigrant and as a citizen.

He was a puddler's assistant in a Pittsburgh iron mill at eleven years of age, and a puddler at sixteen. Born in Wales, he came here with his parents as an immigrant when seven years old. President Harding put the stamp of approval on his citizenship when he placed the great seal of the United States of America on his commission as Secretary of Labor.

When he left the iron and steel business, Mr. Davis became City Clerk of Elwood, Indiana, and he became County Recorder and was successively Director General of the Loyal Order of Moose; founder of Mooseheart Home and School in Illinois and Chairman of the Board of Mooseheart Governors. Under his leadership the list of members in the Order of Moose was increased from a few hundred to 600,000.

Mr. Davis is a member of the Amalgamated Association of Iron and Steel Workers of America, and he is president of a very large and prosperous financial corporation, the American Bond and Mortgage Company of Pittsburgh.

We have no commercial report on him, but the "Literary Digest" recently wrote him up as "Our Millionaire Secretary of Labor."

He is the author of "The Iron Puddler," which Lloyd George said was the most fascinating autobiography he ever read.

It is always a satisfaction and a gratification to meet a man who, even with every help and advantage, has made a success of life, but it is a joy to contemplate a record like this, which has as its foundation a wholesome attitude of mind toward the world and tireless and enthusiastic industry.

I take great pleasure in presenting the Secretary of Labor, Mr. James John Davis.

Labor, Immigration and Citizenship

Address by

Honorable James J. Davis

Secretary of Labor

I must disclaim that affectionate part of the Chairman's introduction as to being a millionaire. The only time I had that experience was when Bill Wrigley turned over Catalina Island to me. I knew then what it meant to be one. After I get out of public office I am going to struggle on to see if I cannot be one.

But I got the name of being a millionaire from a good friend of mine, who did not like me. When I took charge of the Moose organization, when it had just a couple of hundred members, it owed some $50,000, I believe, in bills. We kept on with it, working with it, trying to improve the general tone of the order and its conditions, and I had the pleasure of borrowing for that organization from the kind-hearted gentlemen who preside over the banks of this country nearly $5,000,000. The best part of it is that we paid it all back.

The inception of my getting into the millionaire class in the "Literary Digest" was through this friend of mine who wanted to knock me in a gentlemanly way. He said, "Now, I will show how this fellow Davis has gotten this money." He got hold of a financial statement which showed some $22,587,000. It was the financial statement of the combined lodges of the Moose and the Supreme Lodge, as we term it, including our establishment of Mooseheart out here. He did not know how to read a financial statement very well, so when he saw that he said, "Davis has got $2,250,000, because here it is." That is how I got into the millionaire class.

We have, as the most of you know, out here 1023 acres of the best land in Illinois, and we have expended on those 1023 acres nearly $5,000,000 to try to make the lives of children better, to, as I have said a good many times, give them at least a high school education, but above all, give them a trade. If we are going to shy on anything, I think we will shy on the high school and be sure they have trades. That was my work; that has been my work for a good many years.

I want to take this opportunity of thanking my good friends Fred Upham and Mr. Carry for seeing that I was invited here tonight and getting such a splendid dinner and meeting such a lot of fine fellows. Fred, you have always been kind to me and I hope you will keep it up, and see that I meet this kind of men.

Fred said I ought to tell you about the Department of Labor, because the Department of Labor, as most of you know, was organized to foster, promote and develop the best interests of the wage earners of America and to advance their interests for profitable employment.

In the Department of Labor we have many bureaus and divisions. We have the immigration and naturalization departments, the bureau of labor statistics, the employment service, women in industry, children in industry, and the division of conciliation, together with the finest labor library in the world. Any sort of proposition that you want to find is in that library.

In addition to that we have the housing corporation. That came to us through the war. We operate the ferries at Norfolk, Virginia. We conduct an American plan hotel, which I understand is the largest hotel in the world. We house eighteen hundred women governmental clerks. There is a movement on for the abolishment of the hotel. Fortunately, since we have been in office we made $20,000 or $30,000 the first year and some $90,000 the second year in operating the hotel. Now, that sounds good for a Government ownership, don't you think so, but we did not charge interest on the $2,000,000 or $3,000,000, that was used to build the hotel; some of the overhead is not charged to it, and there are no taxes, or anything of that sort, that a private corporation has to meet, charged to that hotel. So I think it is a fizzle in that respect, so far as Government ownership of a hotel is concerned.

Then we operate the ferries between Norfolk and Portsmouth, Va. In addition to departmental duties, by virtue of the office of Secretary of Labor, I am a member of the Federal Board of Vocational Education. The Federal Board of Vocational Education has to do with appropriating funds to the States, in order to work together with the Government and the corporations for the sole purpose of trying to rehabilitate the disabled men in industry.

We had in the Federal Board when I went into office, charge of the rehabilitation of the disabled soldiers. I remember upon one occasion we needed $140,000,000 to pay off part of the debt of the old administration and to build some new hospitals to take care of disabled soldiers. I went over to the President with it. I was rather nervous, dealing with a $140,000,000 project. It was something new to me. After I talked with the President about the disabled soldiers and told him it was necessary to have his O.K. to go to Charlie Dawes so we could get the money, he said, "Now, it does not make any difference what it takes to rehabilitate the disabled soliders. If it takes all the money that we can rake or scrape together"—I think that was his exact language—"we must find the money to help rehabilitate these boys who were injured in the war."

I thought that was rather encouraging in beginning on that particular line of work.

Then we have the rehabilitation of the disabled men in industry. For my part I believe that, if a man who labors for a great corporation for many years is disabled, it is a part of the Government's duty and the duty of the State and a part of the duty of the corporation to help rehabilitate him and try to put him back into industry. He has some economic value. You can make some use of him, and rather than letting him go about the country begging or asking for charity, there must be some way in which we can work him in and keep him as a useful citizen. That is the work of the Vocational Board.

Then we have the woman in industry. The Woman in Industry Department is the Government's contact with the eight million or more women who are in industry. I believe in taking matters relating to that work with the employer. It has been my policy to go around quietly and talk to the employer, calling his attention to some of the things that we think are not right, with which he is not familiar himself. We get more done that way than by making a lot of noise about it.

I think if a man has something in his factory that is not right and you tell him about it he will correct it, because most of the employers of the country that I have met are fair and square men, want to do what is right, and I have found that the easiest way to get it done is to visit them quietly in their offices, without any blaring of trumpets, but by taking it coolly and calmly and working it out with him.

Then we have the children in industry. The work of the department which takes care of the children in industry has about the same functions as that which handles the women in industry.

So you can see the Department of Labor is the Government's contact with the forty million who are gainfully employed in the United States.

I have often been asked: "What about the wages of working men?" Now, it is not a question of the wages, but it is a question of the cost of living.

I was up home during the Christmas holidays. The old barber, who had been the town barber for some forty years, said to my father, "I don't see you now, Dave, as often as I used to." My father said, "Your hair-cuts now are fifty cents. I remember when you used to cut my hair for fifteen cents and I got a shave from you for a dime."

You must take the wage in proportion with the real cost of living. My friends, I believe it is the best thing for the employees, as I have stated so many times, to have what I term a saving wage. If you reduce the wages of the American working man below a certain standard, what do you have? What does it mean to you? You just take that much out of the purchasing power of the nation.

There is not a manufacturer in America, there is not a business man in America, there is not any one that I know of in America who wants to work for just enough to live on. I say that the man in business ought to have a good return on his money. The manager of the business ought to be paid well and the worker ought to be paid well, because he ought to have enough so that, on Saturday night when he gets his pay, he is able to put a few dollars in the bank to take care of himself and his family on a rainy day.

It is true that it does not make any difference with some men how much money they get; they would not save anything anyway. It is also true that it does not make any difference how much some business men get; they would not save anything either.

Here are these forty millions that are gainfully employed in America. I can best illustrate what I have in mind by telling you something that occurred during the coal controversy. I was asked to go to New York to speak to the manufacturers, and on my way there I stopped off with my people. I said, "Now, what have we got in this home that we did not have in our home in Wales?" We went and looked up every item in the house and I think there were some fifteen different items. I went around the neighborhood and I checked up and asked, "What have you got that you did not have in your homes on the other side?" We had English and we had Irish and we had Polish and we had German and all the rest of them in the neighborhood. I found they had as much as my people had.

Then I said to myself, "What does this mean to the American business man and the American employer?" We are consuming now, or we were at that time, nearly 500,000,000 tons of coal a year. What does it mean to the American business man and to the American merchant if the worker gets the same wage here that he got on the other side, or, if you please, gets the Asiatic wage? What would it mean to the American business man? I can tell you for one thing that a good many stores in that particular town would go out of business, because the retail man would not be needed at all. It would mean that the coal consumption of the United States instead of being nearly 500,000,000 tons would be about 250,000,000 tons, if you shut down all of these factories all over the country and the various agencies which radiate therefrom, such as the transportation industry, if you take out the hauling of that coal and everything connected with it.

I made up my mind then that it was a profitable thing for the great majority of the American business men to see to it that the worker got a good wage, because it meant business for America, because America won't live with cheap labor. A cheap working man will make a cheap employe.

I put this question to my brother, after making a trip around the world: "Where would the big newspapers of America be if they were published, outside of one or two cities, in Asia and Europe? Where would the advertisers be that would print their advertisements? They might put their advertisements in the papers, but the workers would not have enough of a wage to buy what they advertise."

I am not talking about any one class. I figure I am the Secretary of Labor for the forty million who are gainfully employed. There are some inequalities, of course. It is all out of question to talk about some men getting an enormous amount of money for just a little bit of work at the expense of some other workers. I am talking now about the forty millions who are gainfully employed.

What does it mean to the business man if the worker who reads the newspaper has not got the money to buy that which the business man advertises? To my notion, this great cycle revolves around the forty millions who are gainfully employed. That, my friends, is the way I look at it. That is the view I take of it.

As your Chairman has said, I started to work early in life. I have known what my hands can produce. I know what it is to have a father who has worked all these years and saved enough so he is living now in his old age off that which he earned himself, while other men who got the same wage are unfortunately in the poor house. It is the individual himself who must save for himself and must work for himself.

My good friend Llewellyn there, Si Llewellyn of the Interstate Steel Corporation, asked me, "What is the outstanding picture of your boyhood life?" We were talking about things on the other side. I said to Llewellyn that the most beautiful picture that I can recall now—and I have had no reason to change my opinion since—was that of the time when my brother and I used to relieve each other on the puddle furnace.

In those days we worked about eleven hours and a half. We used to get up at two o'clock in the morning, to be there at half past two, to charge the first heat. I worked on one turn and he worked on the other. He was younger than I was. I will never forget those dreary mornings. In those times we had no electric light or any of these other modern conveniences. My mother would get up at two o'clock in the morning to start him off on his day's work. I remember we thought we were well-to-do because we had a red table cloth at that time, and a kerosene lamp. My mother would take that lamp out and would come out and go to the gate and she would sing for him. I would meet him halfway, whistling for him at the mill. Then on my way back she would sing to me in our native tongue, till I got home.

We worked hard. It developed us. My father used to say that hard work would hurt no one if he took his rest. It is the fellow who stays out late who needs the rest and who cannot stand hard work. I realize, of course, that every one needs recreation, but there is usually a time for that.

That, my friends, brings me down to what I am to discuss tonight, immigration and naturalization.

Immigration is the big problem in our department. About 90 per cent of the business, I should think, in the Department of Labor is immigration. Immigration means now more work, with the passage of the three per cent restrictive law, than it did prior to that time when the gates were open.

What is this three per cent restrictive law, most people ask me. Well, it is three per cent of the nationals that were here in 1900. For instance, if there were a thousand Turks here in 1900, only three per cent of that number can come to us. Three per cent is thirty. That means that the Turkish quota is always filled in the first or second month. It is three per cent of the nationals that were here at that time.

In the first three or four months the quotas for a large number of countries are exhausted. I never had anything bring the quota law home more forcefully to me than a telegram which came to me from a city in which there was a discussion, when the Polish quota was exhausted. At that time there was much talk about it. The newspapers had taken it up in every way and they used it as a lever to try to break down this so-called three per cent law. I remember then getting this telegram: "Why let any more Poles in when we have got over 50,000 of them in this city and vicinity that are out of work?"

That rather brought me to my senses and I began looking into the law, getting into the immigration side of it, getting away from the labor side of it and taking up the immigration part.

I found last year that the quotas were exhausted very quickly from the southeastern European countries and what we refer to as "other Asia," but that only fifty per cent of the quotas were exhausted from Great Britain, that is, England, Scotland and Wales, and Norway, Sweden, Denmark, Holland, France and Germany, an average of about fifty per cent. That means more than 100,000 of them could have come from those particular countries, and the year went by leaving that large number to come in from those particular countries.

This year the quota is now exhausted from southeastern Europe. It will not be exhausted from northwestern Europe.

I recently had a discussion with a friend of mine who had been a student in Oxford for some six months, taking a course in economics. One of the things assigned to him was to read the London *Herald*. That is a good job for anybody who wants to take a course in economics, as you will realize if you have ever read it.

When he came back he told me this: "It is a pity. In Wales you have got 20,000 workers who want to come to America. In England you have got 100,000 who want to come to America. In Scotland you have 50,000 who want to come to America; in Norway and Sweden—I was not there, but this is what I understand—there is a large number who want to come from there." I talked with one of the German officials in Washington and he said there is a great army of them in Germany who want to come to America.

Why don't they come in? This country has lost its contact with those people, because immigration ceased to come from there in the middle of the nineties. There is no one to write back home. In the days when we came, my father came out here first and earned enough money to bring us over, his wife and six children.

That contact is lost with northwestern Europe. In addition to that, it costs $80, or somewhere in that neighborhood, if my memory serves me right, for a passport or for the fare to come to this country, the steamship rate. Why, a man, if he came from Germany to this country, would have to take a wheelbarrow to carry enough money to the ticket office to buy a ticket. They have not got the money and that is why they are shut off over there. They have lost the contact with the people here. The quotas of the countries that have not lost the contact are filled in the first two or three months.

You hear many stories about Ellis Island. I have been there on many occasions. I go there because I believe we ought to be kind and generous; we ought to be helpful to them. Most men can come in as immigrants. Those who come within the requirements of the law will not be in Ellis Island three hours before they are through. I have watched it time and again. But what are you going to do when there are six hundred to come in within an hour? They have to be examined. They have to go through all the formalities of the law. So they are detained there. All people who are detained are detained because there is something wrong with them, mental deficiency, contagious, loathsome disease, excess of quota, one or the other thing. We have had as many as 1,600 there at one time. But these people have friends, it seems, in every city in the United States, and they just keep hammering, hammering all the time, through Congressmen and Senators and other friends, and they must manufacture these new stories. My friends, it is not all as I would like to see it, but it is the best we can do under the circumstances.

I take it for granted that it is the wish of every American that, if an incoming baby has a contagious, loathsome disease, it ought to be excluded. I take it that if a person is mentally deficient he ought to be excluded. I take it that every American believes, except maybe one or two of the new recruits to the citizenship, that if a man is an anarchist or a communist or a red, who comes over here for no good purpose, he ought to be excluded.

Sometimes it becomes necessary to separate a child from its mother. This is most painful to me, but it becomes necessary, because the child has ringworm or favus of the scalp or trachoma of the eye. It is a pitiful thing to hear a mother crying out in a strange land because she cannot understand why they are taking her baby to the hospital. The question is, will you send that baby back to the foreign land with some one other than the mother? The mother will never be satisfied to let some one else take it back, so we must insist that the mother go with it.

We have had the experience that a child affected with ringworm of the scalp, or favus, as it is known, was allowed to come in. Of course, in the neighborhood in which it lived numbers of the children of the working class got favus of the scalp. I have seen a hundred of them in a school with ringworm of the scalp.

Are we not to have some sympathy and some regard for the mothers whose children are here just as well as the mothers who are bringing the babies here? It is a terrible ordeal to go through. I have known of a case in which they X-rayed the head until it was as bald as a billiard ball, and on the day I saw it they had to pull them out with pincers. One has this particular picture in mind all the time in the admission of these children. My friends, almost all persons who are detained at Ellis Island are detained because they do not come within the law.

Now, there is a great clamor all over the country. One class is clamoring for putting the bars down and letting everybody come in. There is another class that believes the natural law of fecundity will work it all out, who goes on to say that for every immigrant admitted one child less is born in the United States; that we could have shut off immigration in 1820 and have the same population we are having now, 110,000,000. I am glad they did not shut it off, because I would not be here, and I am glad I am here.

Then you have the other group that believes in putting up the bars altogether and refusing to let anybody come in at all. It is no easy thing for a man to give up his home in a foreign land and start off with his wife and his baby, selling everything he has, to come to this country, only to find he is excluded for some reason or other. It is a most pitiful thing to do. The hangman's job is an easy job compared with mine at times.

So, my friends, for my part I want to express to you my own feeling about this. I believe in this three per cent law, because we have not exhausted the quotas within this three per cent law. I believe that every immigrant, before he starts, ought to be examined and subjected to mental and physical tests. I believe that these examinations or tests ought to be made on the other side, so that when a man comes with his family or comes alone to Ellis Island, we will have nothing but the glad hand for him, make him happy that he is here, and be helpful and kind to him. I do not think there would be much opposition if we made our examinations on the other side.

As it is now we do not have anything to say as to who is going to come here. We have just to take what they give us. We have the metalliferous miners who say they want thirty thousand metalliferous miners in the mines. Then we have the lumbermen, who want ten or fifteen thousand lumberjacks. A lot of factories in the country want common labor. One of the men with whom I was raised in the iron and steel business, who employs thirteen hundred men in the sheet and tin business, told me that he had to have common labor. I asked him why. He said, "We haven't got any." I said, "What is the matter with the soms of those thirteen hundred you have employed? You ought to develop some common labor yourself." He said, "Among the thirteen hundred we have employed there is not one whose sons we can expect to take up a trade, let alone be common laborers."

Is not that a sad commentary on American life? Those are the things that are worthy our thought.

So now, after being with this for nearly two years, I say, why should we throw the bars down? Why should we let a great army come in when we need some metalliferous miners or when we need some lumberjacks? Why let a thousand rug peddlers from Turkey come in, because we want a few common laborers? Why throw the bars down and let everybody come in? The bars are down enough now if they will come.

The reason why they come from the countries where the quotas are now exhausted is because they are well organized and have contact one with the other.

I am informing you of this because, as my friend Fred Upham said, you are the representative business men of Chicago, and I am never afraid to talk to business men, as they are not the kind who insist on the importation of common labor and then let the country go to the dogs; I know they love this country as much as anybody else does. A solicitor from the Department of Labor, whom I asked to go down and make a general survey of this condition, reported that out of six hundred, who went through Ellis Island, it was found only twenty came here for manual labor. A lot of business men think, if they let the bars down, there will rush in all the pick and shovel men they need. This is not so. Again, I say it is all wrong to throw down the bars and let a hundred thousand non-producers come to this country to give us five thousand producers. The time has come when we ought to select the people we want here. Australia just appropriated, I think, some $36,000,000 for working out an immigration program to determine who should come to their country.

If we want common laborers, let us get common laborers. If we want metalliferous miners, let us get metalliferous miners. If we want lumberjacks, let us go to the country which produces lumberjacks, but in order to get the labor we need I do not believe we ought to let down the bars for everybody to come in.

I am for putting up the bars to this country rather than letting everybody in. Make the conditions so that nobody can come in unless he wants to work.

That is the conclusion I have reached, and it is a matter that seems clear to my mind. I am absolutely sincere about it. Why should not these fellows come who are out of work, these sons of the Nordic races? Why should they not come in? There is plenty of work for them to do. No one has any objections to them.

Then, my friends, there is another big problem. The problem of assimilating the immigrant after he gets here. There are some thirteen million immigrants in this country now. Between seven and eight millions of them are unnaturalized. There is a bill in Congress for the enrollment of all aliens, introduced by Senator Shortridge of California and Congressman Johnson of Washington. This bill provides for the enrollment of every alien in America. What for? I talked with two leaders of two different groups. One of them said to me, "Well, we are not going to enroll all the aliens because the employing class will get them." I talked to representatives of the employing class and they said, "We are not going to enroll them because they will be turned into the labor group, into the labor unions." Neither one had thought of what they were going to be as American citizens.

Over in Luzerne County the other day out of 256 men who applied for citizenship, for their second papers,—and they had been here for five to fifteen years,—only 36 were accepted by the Court as competent to be American citizens.

Should we not help them to be American citizens? Should we not be kind to them? Should we not say to them, "We want you to become American citizens"? Should we not teach them the traditions and the early history of this country? Should we not help them so that when the time comes for them to be citizens of this country they will know something about it?

You say that your children must go to school in most of the states, at least, until they are fourteen. You want them to know something about America, but you let the poor alien come in, land in New York City, and do not care where he goes.

There is one hostile crowd that is against the registration of the alien; very hostile, because, in their opinion, it is going to mean an espionage system, such as they had in Europe. This, however, is the farthest from the minds of those who helped to frame the bill. You could not have an espionage system in America with a president. You could not have an espionage system with our Congress and our public men. You would only have in America conditions which would be a help and an assistance to the immigrant.

They say we have now civic organizations that are Americanizing the alien. Yes, but a very small per cent of them come in under it. I do not know anybody that is better able to teach than the civic organizations and under this plan they all come in, with a great national committee at the top of it, and farther down state committees and city committees. There are many, many public men in this room who would serve on these committees for the Americanization of the alien.

As I said on one occasion, we have got to Americanize the alien before the alien alienizes America. We must try to be helpful to them and kind to them, show them the way in America, so that they may have the same opportunity a good many of us have had.

My friends, I am for that bill with all my heart, because I believe it will be helpful to these men.

Let me go back just a minute to this great shortage of labor. There are a million men in America every year who are out of employment. Every day, every year, there are a little over a million of them out of employment. The turnover in some factories is about 100 per cent.

What is the trouble? I will leave that for you to say. I have had some experience with the straw boss and I know he is sometimes in combination with the employment agent, and the more the turnover the better it is for the straw boss. I believe every community could organize in taking care of its common labor. If we had a national organization through which it could function, I believe that every church, every fraternal organization, every civic organization and every other kind of organization would be interested in that employment agency, or should be interested. Most men are afraid to go to an employment agency because they have to pay for it. If there is anything in America that ought to be free, it ought to be the place where a man can go and get a job.

How many men have you in Chicago tonight that have come from the great Northwest who are sleeping in some of the bed houses on Clark Street, who would like to have a job if they had the opportunity, if there was some organization to which they could apply so they could go to work? Of course, I know there are a lot of loafers, poor loafers and rich loafers, who will never work, and you will never make them work. It has got to be born in a fellow, otherwise he won't work.

So, my friends, getting back to this immigration proposition again, I want to make it just as clear to you as I possibly can that after my experience I am for this selective plan of examination on the other side, and when the immigrant comes here let us make him feel as though he is somebody, and let us not suffer him simply to go where his nose leads him. We ought to help him and see that he is started right.

Now let me discuss a subject I want to close with. This friend of mine who just came back from Great Britain, whom I mentioned a short while ago as having taken a course at

Oxford, informed me that a great labor leader told him that the birth rate in Great Britain exceeds the death rate every year by 250,000; that since 1913, although they lost some 900,000 during the war, their population has increased by more than a million people; that for every seven jobs in Great Britain they have ten men to fill them; that it is worrying the government; that a good many men over in that section of the country are preaching this sort of doctrine: "Don't go to the colonies; don't go away from here to work. Let us stay here and at the end we will create so much dissatisfaction and discontent that we will run the government." A fine-looking government a lot of discontenters could run! I have never seen anybody who was discontented who could run anything. That has been my experience in dealing with men for nearly thirty years over this country.

Some one has to lead in a movement to stimulate the coming to us of the representatives of the old so-called Nordic races. Something extraordinary must be done. I leave that to you.

So, my friends, let us be kind to these men. Let us be generous to these men when they come. Let us help these men when they are here as aliens. Let us not forget them the day they land in New York or Chicago and say they can go wherever they want. Let us not have people going around taking up collections from the big business men in the country and from everybody else, passing the hat everywhere, to Americanize the alien. Let him pay a little fee, five or ten dollars. The bill provides in this enrollment of aliens that every dollar the alien expends he gives for himself. It is going to be helpful to him. We have also provided that, if one is too poor and his wages are not high enough, we have got the right through the naturalization officer to remit it to him.

Let us be kind to them, so that the contemplated enrollment will become a powerful influence against that hostile crowd that is now going into the interior towns, into the congested parts of great cities, preaching the doctrine of hate, preaching the doctrine of revolution, preaching the doctrine of installing a new kind of government, in which only a certain class can be represented. This America will never amount to anything if any class runs it. This America will never be the America we want it to be if everybody has not the same rights as others under our Constitution.

This crowd that is always at work preaching the doctrine of revolution and hate, preaching the doctrine of overthrow, will oppose this enrollment plan. The other day I heard of one who had five hundred in his audience, making statements of which not a line was true. He had them worked up so that, when he passed the hat, they gave him practically all they had. I think there must have been about $125 in the hat. Then he had the nerve to say to them, "You have only given me $125 and I am doing all this for you."

What was he doing? Prejudicing them against the Government; prejudicing them against their employers; prejudicing them against every business man and every associate who is a higher man.

Besides, there is something just coming to my mind. What are we going to do if we do not have common labor in America. What will we do with the mechanics? That is an all-important question. Shall the mechanics step down and be common laborers? Thus you will realize the enrollment of the alien and this immigration bill are two of the most important bills that are now pending in Congress so far as the future of America is concerned.

Listen to what a distinguished member of a certain east European racial group is quoted as having said recently: "This country is not a nation; it is a gathering of peoples from every corner of the earth. No one racial group, no matter how early settled in this country, can furnish more than one note in this vast symphony of nations."

This means only one thing. It means that this new American and his followers believe that there is no real America. It means that the history of this country, its traditions, its civilization, will be forgotten. It means that the term "American" as applied to our people will not exist. It means that this great country, stretching from sea to sea, is to be a mere jumble of racial groups, preserving their racial customs, and their racial languages, without common interests or common ideals. It means that the whole fabric of social, economic, and political life, built through the toil and sorrow and suffering of the last one hundred and fifty years on this continent, is to be shattered. It means that the principles of union and liberty, for which millions have laid down their lives, shall perish in a welter of discord like unto that which fell upon Babel.

That is not the America I know. It is not, I trust, the America that my children will know. My people did not come to this country with any such America in mind. My father came here to better his condition in life, and by hard toil he accomplished his purpose. He came to become an American, and to bring up his family in that equality of opportunity which America meant to him and them.

When as a lad of eight years I followed my mother, as with her six children she led the way from the shadows of the old Castle Garden immigrant station at the Battery, I came to a new life. She did not bring her brood here to preserve in them a miniature reproduction of the land she had left behind. Raising her eyes to the wonders of Broadway, to the towering buildings that typified the greatness of the land that lay beyond them, she cried out with tears in her eyes: "This is the land I long have sought."

She visioned her sons as part and parcel of this great new civilization that stretched out before her. She mourned not for what she had left behind. On the threshold of the United States, all that was about her of the Old World fell away, and she and her children faced the future, not as foreigners, not as aliens, but as Americans, Americans in heart and Americans in soul.

I say to you, gentlemen, that when those who come to us from abroad fail to consecrate themselves wholly and entirely to America, to American life, to American institutions, we have lost the thing which has made this a great nation. I say to you that the man who comes from abroad bringing only his hands and his head and leaving his heart and his loyalty behind him, is not fit for a place among us.

When new Americans talk of racial groups sounding but a single note in the symphony of America, I say to them that America can be no symphony. America can be but a single note, a clarion call, sounding aloud to all the world the eternal principles of liberty under law, of the rights of humanity. We have no divided allegiance in our citizenship, no double loyalty. An American must be for America against all the world.

Summing up what I have said to you, I want to say, so far as I am concerned, that I am endeavoring to do all I can to create sentiment for these things. I stand for this enrollment of the alien bill and I stand for selective immigration. I stand for examinations on the other side. I stand for the thing that will bring men to America who will come here to work and help to do things that will make this country greater and better than it ever has been.

I am glad of this opportunity to be able to express myself to you, the business men of this community, and again I thank my friend Fred Upham and my friend Mr. Carry for inviting me to this place tonight through the President of this Club.

MR. HARRY A. WHEELER: Mr. President, I wish to move a vote of thanks to the Secretary of Labor for his address, in expression of appreciation for his coming to us to-night from Washington to make that delivery.

President Sunny: You have all heard the motion. Is there a second?

(There were many seconds, and on a viva voce vote the motion was unanimously carried.)

TWO HUNDRED AND EIGHTY-FIFTH REGULAR MEETING

CHICAGO CLUB

FRIDAY, FEBRUARY 9, 1923

Closed Meeting:

TWO HUNDRED AND EIGHTY-SIXTH REGULAR MEETING

THE CONGRESS

FRIDAY, MARCH 9, 1923

Open Meeting: President B. E. Sunny Presiding

Invocation: Reverend Norman Hutton

ADDRESS

WORLD COMMUNICATIONS.

BRIGADIER GENERAL JOHN J. CARTY

Vice-President in Charge of the Department of Development and Research of the American Telegraph & Telephone Company.

PRESIDENT B. E. SUNNY: Ladies and Gentlemen: The telephone has been in almost universal service for so long that it is difficult to believe that, in the beginning, it was regarded as an interesting scientific discovery rather than a device of commercial and domestic utility, and capital to promote it, and subscribers to the service, were hard to secure.

Its application to everyday use had to be worked out by men with no previous experience, and for the first three or four years, the results were not satisfactory. The service was slow; the wires were noisy, and talking was possible only when the distances were comparatively short.

Instructions to subscribers printed in the Chicago Telephone Directory of June 1, 1879, when there were about three hundred and fifty telephones, give an interesting picture of the equipment and service at that time:

"First: To call the exchange office to which your wire runs, push up the knob underneath the call bell—hold it up while you give one or two turns to the crank (which is enough). If everything is right, your own bell will ring too.

"Second: The exchange office will answer by a short ring at your bell. Then state your name and that of the party you want, unhooking telephone while you talk. Hang up your telephone, and wait till notified by long ring that your party is being rung up. If he is in his office and answers the call, you will find him at the other end of the line at once. If he does not answer the first ring, the exchange operator will call him again.

"When through talking, hang up your telephone and give one short ring for disconnection. This ring should always be given by the party asking for connection.

"Note: Parties having a switch on their bell—boxes instead of a hook—must remember to turn the switch to the right when talking; at all other times invariably to the left.

"A ticket is made at exchange office for each connection asked for. Unless connection is delayed over ten minutes, do not repeat the call when your connection is not made instantly—because it simply piles up more than one ticket, for but one connection, and creates confusion."

Incidentally, it is an interesting fact that this telephone directory was the first to print numbers in front of the names, but you will have noticed that in the rules I have read, subscribers were not asked to call by number. Indeed, the opposition to the use of numbers was so great the idea had to be dropped and the numbers were omitted in the next directory. Subsequently when there were five or six hundred subscribers, numbers had to be insisted upon.

There were less than 5,000 telephones in Chicago in 1887, ten years after the exchange was started, and 28,000 in 1900; in 1910, 240,000; and now 648,000.

It might be said that it required the first twenty years to get rid of the knobs, switches, and bell cranks; to clear the wire of noises; to develop speedy and accurate switching apparatus; to find out how to make cables for underground work to replace the masses of wires in the streets and on the roofs.

The conditions in Chicago in 1879, as outlined, were about the same as elsewhere, and it was in that year that our distinguished guest began his telephone career in Boston, operating a switchboard for $5 a week. The mysticism and romance that lay back of the cords and plugs and tangled wires, and the obvious crudity and inadequacy of the apparatus, made a strong appeal to the imagination and ingenuity with which he was generously endowed, and since then, while he has always been a loyal family man, we sometimes suspect that the telephone with him is "next of kin."

In his enthusiastic zeal, he seemed to regard the infantile maladies of the telephone a personal challenge, which he at once accepted. He worked and preached early and late for their elimination. He made important inventions and discoveries, but, more than that, he was the inspirer of great discoveries and inventions by others. The universal system of verbal communication is the product of many scientists, engineers and inventors, but Carty, whose labor spans the life-time of the telephone, and whose patience, courage and vision is associated with the solution of almost all of the big problems, will be accorded generous and grateful acknowledgment.

Bell made the telephone talk. Carty made it talk so we could understand it!

Professor Michelson, speaking of his own great achievement, says: "Those things that look rather big at the time are the result of desultory thinking, that finally all comes together."

When the war came, the desultory thinking of Carty for almost forty years took immediate and substantial form in the organization of a personnel, and the marshaling of electrical appliances and devices for the aid, support and protection of lives and property.

He became a major in the Signal Officers' Reserve Corps in January and was promoted to colonel in August, 1917, and served in France from July, 1918 to May, 1919.

The signal corps of the A. E. F. comprised 147 battalions of 54,000 men.

It built, almost over night, complete telephone exchanges for the huge cantonments for the newly created hosts of the national army. It supplied a technically trained personnel for the signal service, for administrative, for front line duty, for the navy, for special wire radio, for anti-submarine service, and the dozen other branches of the military and naval activity.

It built in France a complete American system of telephone and telegraph with devices and methods of which Europe had scarcely dreamed. It pushed its work under shell and machine-gun fire, supplying wire communication that linked the onrushing infantry to its base of command and supply.

It bent the creative thought of a large corps of highly trained inventors to new and uncanny military devices, which widened the range of wireless speech, aided the navy to track submarines; located the direction of enemy gun fire and of hostile air craft maneuvering in the dark.

It is said that wherever General Pershing stopped, there was a telephone at his service to put him in quick communication with his staff and the allied armies.

The war over, Carty was communications officer of the Peace Commission, and in December, 1921, he was made a brigadier general in the Officers' Reserve Corps.

His services were further recognized by the Distinguished Service Medal of the United States, and his designation by France as an Officer of the Legion of Honor.

I take very great pleasure in introducing General John J. Carty, who will address us on the subject of "World Communications."

World Communications:

Address by

Brigadier General John J. Carty,

Vice-President in Charge of the Development and Research of the American Telephone and Telegraph Company.

Mr. President and Ladies and Gentlemen: I am introducing you to a new apparatus, such as was employed by President Harding when he was inaugurated. On that day he was easily heard by the largest audience that had ever listened to an orator, 125,000 people.

Perhaps you are not aware that my voice is receiving much help from this apparatus. Although this is a small auditorium I think it will be noticeable if I cut it off, at least in the distant parts of the room. I have a little button to my right, and when I press it, it will cut off the apparatus, and when I release it the apparatus will be put on again. The apparatus is now on, and when I press the button now the apparatus is off. Now the apparatus is on again. I will count while the apparatus is on and while it is off. Now it is off. One, two, three, four, five. One, two, three, four, five. I think perhaps you all notice it.

With such an apparatus as this a great many remarkable things can be done, and it is destined to work a revolution in oratory. Let us take a field, a square field, three thousand feet on each side. If you allowed in such a field as that just four square feet for each individual, you could stand in it two and one-fourth million people. If I were standing in the middle of that field, equipped as I am now, I could be heard with perfect ease by each one of those two and one-fourth million people. They would all hear me just exactly as you now hear me.

If you could gather all the population of Chicago into a large field, it would be perfectly easy to make them all hear, just as you hear me now; and if we had several fields in different parts of the United States, or one in each of the states, gathering the populations of the states in those fields, we could connect them together by wire, as we shall do tonight, and all of them could hear my voice just as easily as you are hearing me now.

The other night, as I shall say in my address, I was talking to an audience in London. I was in New York. They were not able to answer back over there, because they have not yet got the American appliances. So we provided a cable for that purpose. I had been out very late many evenings preparing for the test, and my throat was rather bad. I was not speaking very well, so I was being criticized from London in some such fashion as this—imagine where I was talking, a distance of almost 3000 miles—"Carty, you are slurring every syllable. Dwell longer on your final syllables." That was what I was getting from my London audience.

I endeavored to clear my throat, the only thing I could think of doing, to brace up a little bit, and I inadvertently coughed, and, as I shall tell you later, that cough was heard in London. I became a celebrated man. The longest cough in the world, three thousand miles. That will give you some idea of the instrumentalities which we have here tonight.

Now, my topic is "World Communications." It is a very large subject, but I will try to keep it within the compass of a short time.

Of all the agencies employed in the electrical communications of the world, the telephone is the most wonderful.

Tonight I shall speak of its achievements and possibilities. The telephone art, more than any other, is a product of American institutions and reflects the genius of our people. The story of its development is a story of our own country, of American enterprise and American progress, for although the most powerful governments of Europe have been engaged in the development and operation of telephone systems, no great contribution to the art has been made by any of them. The best that is used in telephony throughout the world is American, and it is manufactured here in Chicago in the great works at Hawthorne. There is located the largest industrial establishment in Chicago, and by far the greatest manufactory of communications material to be found anywhere upon the earth. This institution, now providing work for 30,000 of your population, was founded by a distinguished business man of Chicago who was for many years an Active Member of this Club—the late Enos M. Barton.

Throughout the world, among those engaged in electrical communications, no city is of greater interest than Chicago. From all the civilized countries of the earth, government departments of communications as well as communications companies send their experts to Chicago to observe, in the making, such marvels of equipment as we shall see in operation tonight.

For another reason these experts from abroad come here to study the telephone art. Chicago is situated at the center of the great telephonic trunk line—a marvel of scientific construction—which carries the tones of the human voice from Cuba to California. From Chicago radiate in all directions great telephone nerves of communication which extend throughout the continent, connecting together fourteen million stations, and rendering service to a hundred million people. The telephone system of Chicago itself is an electrical complex of wires and stations resembling an immense nerve ganglion, vitalizing the activities of this great city upon which the commerce, the agriculture, and the industries of the country and of the world so much depend. Within the city of Chicago alone, there are more telephones than in any of France, and more than are to be found in Australia, Italy, Belgium and Switzerland combined. Chicago has more telephones than London, Paris, Rome, Brussels, and The Hague added together.

With the products of Chicago manufacture, Americans have constructed in our own country an electrical system of communications of transcendent magnitude and usefulness. They have made the telephone into a powerful agency for the advancement of civilization, eliminating barriers to speech, binding our people into one nation, and now reaching out to the uttermost limits of the earth.

The idea that a world system will some day be established is not employed merely to create an interest in what I shall have to say tonight. From the beginning, it has been an article of faith with the telephone pioneers. In the charter of an American telephone company, written in the early days of the art, you will find it set down in calm, legal phraseology as the ultimate objective of a company of farseeing American men of business. At the time that this charter was written none of the great improvements which we have made since had been accomplished, and telephone service from New York to Boston, and even from New York to Philadelphia was unknown. Indeed, talking through underground cables for more than a few miles was impracticable. From this remarkable charter, I shall read but one clause, as follows:

"And it is further declared and certified that the general route of the lines of this association, in addition to those hereinbefore described or designated, will connect one or more points in each and every city, town or place in the state of New York with one or more points in each and every other city, town or place in said state, and in each and every other of the United States, and in Canada and Mexico; and each and every of said cities, towns and places is to be connected with each and every other city, town or place in said states and countries, and also by cable and other appropriate means with the rest of the known world."

When these words were written we had wire and cables, and now, marvelous to relate, in the new art of radio we have, exactly as foreshadowed in the charter, the "other appropriate means."

Nowhere in history can there be found such faith as this on the part of business men in the possibilities of science, and nowhere can there be found a record of such confidence in the scientific men upon whose work they based their expectations. After what you will see and hear tonight, I am sure that you will agree with me that never before has the business man's belief in the possibilities of science been so splendidly justified, and that never before has his faith in organized, co-operative, human effort been followed by such a fulfillment. It should be an inspiration to all men of business and to all men of science to see, in the progress of the telephone art, the marvelous results which can be attained when scientific effort is combined with sound business management. So striking, indeed, are these results, that it is now coming to be recognized that a department for scientific research is an indispensable part of a modern industrial organization. So true is this, that competent authorities now believe that those concerns which do not establish such a department and thus take advantage of the boundless possibilities of science, cannot succeed in competition with those that do.

It is difficult to appreciate how rapid is the progress of science in this age, and how revolutionary are the changes it can make in commerce and industry and in our daily lives even during one generation. It was only a few months ago that Alexander Graham Bell who invented the telephone and who spoke the first words through it, died. The man who made the first telephone for Bell, who was the first telephone engineer, and who ran the first telephone line and heard the first words spoken over it, is still alive. He is not much over sixty years old. I refer to Dr. Thomas A. Watson. He is not present with us tonight in person, nor will he speak to us by radio, nor by the long distance wires. Nevertheless, by man's scientific control over the forces of nature, we can see his moving form and listen to his spoken words, and what we shall see and hear of him tonight will be seen and heard long after he and we are dead. This will exemplify the telephone and the phonograph, inventions of two Americans, Bell and Edison, whose names will be remembered as long as men can speak and as long as men can hear. There is no better way to understand the beginning of the telephone art than to let Dr. Watson tell us in his own words what happened on the day and at the very moment the telephone was born.

We will now hear Dr. Watson. (There was then exhibited a remarkable talking moving picture entitled, "The Birth of the Telephone," by Mr. Thomas A. Watson, who, while the picture was being shown, made the following remarks:)

Ladies and Gentlemen: In 1874 I first met Alexander Graham Bell, who came to the shop where I was working to have his harmonic telegraph constructed. This work was assigned to me. The object of his invention was the transmission of several (telegraph) messages over one wire at the same time, utilizing the fact that a tuned reed will vibrate when its own note is sounded near it.

This is a receiver of Bell's telegraph with its magnet and steel reed. The transmitter had, in addition, contact points which, when its reed vibrated, would send corresponding electric impulses through the distant receiver. If that receiver's reed was tuned to the pitch of those pulsations, it would respond.

I made for Bell six transmitters with reeds of six different pitches, and six receivers with their reeds tuned to correspond.

The apparatus didn't work very well. Bell was obliged constantly to retune the receiver reeds. When doing this he had the habit of pressing the receiver against his ear. This led to a most important discovery.

During the months we were experimenting on his telegraph, Bell often spoke to me of another invention he was struggling with. It was the telephone. I remember my surprise when he first told me he expected soon to be able to talk by telegraph. He explained to me his wonderful idea of an electric current, which would copy the vibrations of speech, and described a complex telephone he had devised. It was never constructed as it was too expensive.

June 2, 1875, is the most important day in the history of the telephone, for on that day Bell got a glimpse that showed him the road leading to the realization of his speaking telephone idea.

That afternoon, his harmonic telegraph was working worse than ever. One of the steel reeds in my room stopped vibrating. I snapped it several times to start it when Bell came rushing from the other room in great excitement. He told me that he had heard in the receiver at his ear the actual sound of the spring I had snapped. It was the first real sound that had ever been transmitted to a human ear by electricity and he was sure that the same mechanism would also transmit speech. The telephone was really born at that instant, for that very afternoon Bell gave me directions for making the first speaking telephone. This is an exact duplicate of it. It has one of the telegraph receivers set in a frame with the free end of its reed attached to the center of a drumhead and a mouthpiece to talk into. Bell's idea was to force the reed to follow the voice vibrations instead of merely swinging to and fro.

I made two of these telephones the next day and we tested them on the evening of June 3, 1875. I could hear the sound of Mr. Bell's voice and could almost understand some of his words, but my voice was not strong enough to make him hear a sound. He was disappointed but he was sure that he was on the right track.

Many experiments on the telephone followed during the next two years. Here are a few of the many telephones I made for Bell during that period.

On March 10, 1876, the telephone transmitted its first complete sentence—"Mr. Watson, please come here; I want you."

On October 9, 1876, the first conversation over a real wire was carried on by Mr. Bell and myself. It was two miles long, running from Boston to Cambridge.

The telephone was ready for public use in the spring of 1877, two years after the first telephone was made. This is one of the first telephones put into commercial use.

General Carty: Dr. Watson has now told us of the first crude telephone. You are all familiar with the modern instrument which every business man has on his desk. This instrument is the simplest element of an inconceivably complex electrical system of communications. But, simple as it appears to the eye, this instrument is not so simple after all. By means of another scientific device representing man's rapidly advancing power to utilize the forces of nature, I shall show you how complex it really is.

We will now have the telephone picture. (An interesting short film was then shown, demonstrating the assembling of a telephone instrument.)

General Carty: Those are simply a couple of cocktails to carry us through some rather dreary speaking for a while.

Even this picture is not sufficient to give more than a hint of the marvels contained in this instrument which is the simplest part of the vast telephone system which is at our service day and night. Volumes could be written about it, and even then there would be more to tell. Among the parts which were displayed on the screen there were many substances among which were rubber and asphaltum from South America, platinum from Russia, silk from Japan, wool from Australia, cotton from the South, coal and iron from Pennsylvania, lead from Missouri, linen from Ireland, mica and shellac from India, copal from Africa, nickel from Canada, and even gold from Alaska.

But another marvelous thing about this telephone instrument can be seen only at that vast industrial establishment where it is made. There, we can see these crude, inanimate materials, which are formed out of the dust of the earth, being transmuted by miracles of science into something which almost seems to be alive, for we speak to it, and we can hear it speak. By the words which we hear from it, we are coming more and more to regulate our daily lives. More than any of us realize, it has transformed our business methods and expanded our social life. So rapid has been the growth of the telephone service, and so diffused have been its effects, that their magnitude and far-reaching importance have not yet been perceived. Even before the death of its founder, Alexander Graham Bell, the telephone art, after less than fifty years of its development, had provided a system of intercommunication which we are now only just beginning to see is an indispensable element in that stupendous evolution which society is now undergoing.

Time does not permit me to make more than brief mention of some of the achievements of science exemplified in telephone progress since that historic day when the telephone was born. On January 25, 1915, the transcontinental line, spanning Bell's adopted country from ocean to ocean, was, in the presence of dignitaries of State and Nation, dedicated to the public service. This was a day of triumph for Bell, for, using a reproduction of the original instrument, he again spoke the memorable words, "Mr. Watson, come here; I want you." But this time Bell was at New York, and Watson who heard him with perfect ease, was three thousand miles away in San Francisco.

Another advance attained the greatest distance over which the transmission of speech had ever been achieved, nearly eight years ago. Early in the morning of September 30, 1915, words were spoken through a radio telephone at Arlington, Virginia, to the Hawaiian Islands, where they were plainly heard. But, as if to proclaim the telephonic conquest of time as well as space, the words reached these distant islands of the Pacific when it was there still the evening of September 29.

There yet remained to be realized that prophetic dream of the telephone pioneers, the bridging of the Atlantic by the human voice. But the day of its fulfillment was not far off, for on October 21, 1915, during the dark days of the war, speech was, for the first time in history, successfully transmitted across the Atlantic Ocean. This was accomplished by the radio telephone, which carried the words spoken at Arlington to the Eiffel Tower at Paris.

While these achievements definitely secured for American scientists the record of being the first to transmit speech by radio telephone across the Atlantic Ocean and across the North American continent and out into the Pacific as far as Hawaii, it was only brief sentences that were transmitted, and these only after months of trial. These results are not as great in technical importance as those obtained during our recent talking from New York to London, in which speech transmission was so successful that the voices of all of the speakers were heard loudly and distinctly and were clearly recognized. This talking was continued during a period of exactly two hours, following to the minute a program which had been determined in advance.

I was one of the speakers, and in endeavoring to clear my throat, I inadvertently coughed in front of the transmitter. This was loudly heard by the audience in London and the London morning newspapers in large type announced that I was the first one whose cough had been heard across the Atlantic.

Another memorable telephone development will always be associated with a great historic occasion. At the burial of the Unknown Soldier at Arlington, on November 11, 1921, the voice of President Harding, by means of the new loud speaking amplifiers, which I am using tonight, was easily heard by the great concourse of a hundred thousand people about him, even by those in the most distant parts of the vast cemetery. Corresponding multitudes numbered by tens of thousands at New York and San Francisco, heard over the wires every word spoken by their chief magistrate, as clearly as though in his actual presence. These distant multitudes heard also the invocation of the chaplain, the music and the hymns, and the words of the commitment service used by the bishop at the grave. They joined with each other and with those at the cemetery in the singing of the hymns, and they united with the President in reciting the Lord's Prayer, with which he closed his address. They heard in amazement the salvos of artillery fired at the grave, and even those on the shores of the Pacific caught the loud reverberations thrown back by the Virginia hills. At the end, in profound silence and with heads bowed in sorrow, they listened to the plaintive notes of the trumpet sounding the soldiers' last farewell. On that day, the achievements of science imparted a mystical power to the most solemn national ceremony in the history of America.

These are but some of the advances which have been made in the first half century of the telephone art. They show the great and rapid progress which man has made in a short time in the evolution of powers outside of his own body.

But these advances have been made only because equally great progress has been made in the evolution of the group mind, in the co-ordination and conscious direction of larger and larger numbers of men towards a predetermined objective.

The laboratory which originally contained but one worker, Bell, and then two, Bell and Watson, now contains thousands representing various departments of physical science. Great ideas must come from the mind of an individual genius like Bell, or Edison, or Pupin, but to apply the idea to such a complex entity as a telephone system, the countless parts of which cover a continent, no individual unaided can bring it to a successful practical application. The co-operative work of a comprehensive and effective scientific organization is necessary, and years of expensive work are required before the idea can be rendered useful to society.

But more than this is required in order to construct and operate and maintain and manage such a vast system of telephone intercommunication as that of the United States. An immense organization depending upon the co-operation of hundreds of thousands of minds distributed throughout the land has been evolved. As illustrating the development of man's powers outside of his own body and the development of the group mind, the telephone art and the telephone organization are regarded today as outstanding examples of the endless possibilities of human evolution.

Since I was invited to address the members of this Club, we have made such improvements in the methods of transmitting speech by wire that it would now be possible to talk all the way around the world by means of wires strung upon poles, if the land could be found upon which to erect them. Unfortunately, the problem of talking through long submarine cables such as would be required across the ocean, yet remains to be solved. But, as if to make up for this deficiency, it is since I was invited to address you that we talked so successfully from New York to London by radio.

This brings us to the consideration of the fascinating subject of the possibilities of radio in the grand scheme of world communications. We must first distinguish between the radio telegraph and the radio telephone. It is a much simpler problem to operate the radio telegraph over great distances than it is to talk by the radio telephone. Both are subject to interference from other stations, and both are subject to interference by those natural noises which are called statics or atmospherics. In addition to being very much more complicated than the telegraph, the radio telephone requires from six to ten times as large a band of wave lengths in the ether as does the telegraph. In other words, the available facilities of the ether permit a much smaller number of simultaneous telephone messages than telegraph messages.

Before the advent of the radio telegraph, there was no very effective means of communicating with ships and other moving stations, and it is by virtue of the inherent character of all radio messages—that they spread out in all directions—that the wireless telegraph has greatly increased the safety of travel at sea, becoming a blessing to the mariner and those who entrust themselves to his care.

In addition to its uses in navigation, the wireless telegraph has taken its place beside the submarine cable as a means of transoceanic telegraph communication. The wireless telegraph finds its best field across large bodies of water such as the Atlantic and Pacific oceans where the only wire communication possible is by means of submarine cables which work very inefficiently as compared to land cables of the same length. Across the ocean, the relative advantage of the telegraph cable and the radio telegraph are difficult to appraise. Each has advantages over the other, and each has its disadvantages, and each is carrying its share of the international telegraph traffic of the world.

While the radio telegraph does not function as successfully over large areas of land as over corresponding areas of water, the telegraph cable over land is vastly more efficient than is the deep-sea submarine cable of an equal length. The submarine cable consists of one conductor, whereas the long distance land cable, although less than three inches in diameter, may contain as many as 600 conductors. Such a cable, when constructed and operated in accordance with the latest scientific discoveries, can be made to carry as many as fifteen thousand telegraph messages at one time, as compared with only two messages carried at one time by the submarine cable.

While the number of land cables may be increased without limit and can carry volumes of traffic immeasurably in excess of that which could ever be required, the number of messages which radio can carry at one time is restricted, due to the fact that each radio message tends to spread out in all directions, thus traveling through the same region in which many other messages are traveling.

The best field for the radio telegraph is for long distance, transoceanic communication; for the radio compass, by means of which the navigator at sea can get his true bearings from radio stations on the shore; for time signals; for auxiliary radio fog signals given out by lighthouses; and for many military and naval purposes; and for transmitting messages to and from ships and other moving stations, and between places where wires are not available. In all of these situations, there is a great future for the radio telegraph.

And now, as to the radio telephone. At the present time the public are much interested in the radio telephone because it is used in broadcasting, that is, the sending out from a central station of speeches, phonograph records, musical performances, and the like, to be heard by incredible numbers who are equipping themselves with radio telephone receiving apparatus adapted to this class of service. These broadcast messages, as well as all radio messages, are carried by the ether, which may be likened to a universal party-line consisting of a single conductor which must be used in common by all the world. Although ingenious methods have been devised whereby the number of simultaneous radio messages carried by this party-line, the ether, may be largely increased, even then it can at best carry only a small fraction of the total world traffic.

In addition to this limitation on the number of conversations which may be carried simultaneously, the radio telephone is peculiarly subject to atmospheric electrical disturbances, more so than the telegraph. At times these disturbanecs are violent, particularly where high amplification is required as in transoceanic radio. In such cases they interfere with conversation for hours and even days at a time. They are more prevalent in the summer than in the winter season, and in the tropics than in the higher latitudes. Unless we overcome this most formidable problem presented by the atmospheric disturbances, even this relatively limited use of the radio telephone will be still further restricted. This problem of atmospheric disturbance has baffled the scientists of all the world, and some are beginning to think that it is something like the problem of overcoming the weather.

Mark Twain once said that people are always complaining about the weather, but no one ever seems to do anything about it. As the summer approaches, more and more people are complaining about the statics, but nobody yet seems to have been able to do much about it. Frequently in the daily press we read announcements that a remedy has been found for statics. But the remedy must have been something like the Keeley cure. A man was once asked whether he thought the Keeley cure was a good thing. He replied that it was, and a very fine thing, for had it not cured him four times! Although "cured" of the statics, many times, the radio operators are still hearing things they don't want to hear.

Aside from these static difficulties, there is the interference problem caused by the increasing number of sending stations which produce such great confusion in the ether, and which has already been referred to. This problem is receiving the attention of many of the governments of the world, and more particularly of our own. It is a problem of national and international regulation by law. Some idea of the situation may be gained from a public statement by Secretary Hoover, made after the appointment of a board of government experts to consider the whole subject. In the course of this statement, Secretary Hoover said:

"I think that it will be agreed at the outset that the use of the radio telephone for communication between single individuals as in the case of the ordinary telephone is a perfectly hopeless notion. Obviously if ten million telephone subscribers are crying through the air for their mates they will never make a junction; the ether will be filled with frantic chaos, with no communication of any kind possible."

Thus the characteristics of radio messages causing them to spread out over large areas, enabling the radio telephone to be of inestimable service in certain fields, is one of the factors which stand in the way of its general use as a substitute for wires. Scientists long ago demonstrated that wires are nothing more nor less than pathways for guiding or directing the electric waves in the ether between any desired points, however numerous they may be or wherever they may be situated. By means of these wire guides, millions upon millions of messages may be carried simultaneously without interference with each other.

It has often been said that had the course of scientific development been reversed so that radio transmission preceded transmission by wire, the discovery that wires can be used to guide the ether waves would be considered one of the marvels of science. By their use, the otherwise uncontrolled ether waves are caused to follow any predetermined pathway, flashing hundreds of thousands of messages to and fro under our city streets without the slightest interference, each message following its allotted course, whether up through the intricate structure of a thirty-story office building, or out across the plains, under rivers and over mountains, even to the far side of the continent, there to be received by him, and him alone, for whom it is intended.

The natural characteristics of radio and wire transmission are, therefore, fundamentally different. Each, due to its unique capabilities, is performing a service for which the other is unsuited, and each is supplementing the other to the end that there may be provided all the facilities necessary to extend throughout the whole world a comprehensive system of electrical communications. For the large amounts of traffic on land, both telegraph and telephone, which must be handled with certainty and a minimum of cost, the use of wires is necessary. But as an agency for communicating over wide stretches of water, with moving conveyances generally, for numerous maritime and military purposes, and for the broadcasting of information, and in other situations where wires are not available, radio telephony is capable of rendering services of unique importance.

When all of these necessary services are provided for, the capacity of the ether for conveying messages simultaneously without interference, will be taxed to the limit. Therefore, the ether must be reserved exclusively for those services for which wires are not adapted. Fortunately, these services comprise but a small fraction of the future world communications. If we had to depend upon radio alone, mankind could never realize the incalculable benefits which are destined to grow out of a comprehensive system of worldwide communications. The ultimate system which is to provide the communications of the world will consist of both wire and radio, each supplementing the other in proportion to its capabilities. By far the largest part of this world communications service must be carried by wire.

And now, before we proceed to our demonstration, let me say a few words concerning the broader aspects of our subject. We are only just beginning to appreciate how fundamental are electrical communications in the organization of society. We are as yet unable to appreciate how vital they are to the ultimate welfare of mankind.

The use of the spoken word to convey ideas, distinguishes man from all other created things. The extension of the spoken word by means of electrical systems of intercommunication serves to connect the nervous system of each unit of society with all of the others, thus providing an indispensable element in the structure of that inconceivably great and powerful organism which modern science tells us is to be the ultimate outcome of the stupendous evolution which society is undergoing.

I believe that some day we will build up a great world telephone system, making necessary to all the nations the use of a common language or a common understanding of languages, which will join all the people of the earth into one brotherhood. When, by the aid of science and philosophy and religion, man has prepared himself to receive the message, we can all believe there will be heard throughout the earth a great voice coming out of the ether, which will proclaim, "Peace on earth, good will towards men." Then will be realized that vision so beautifully described by the poet:

"Wherein each earth-encircling day shall be
A Pentecost of speech, and men shall hear,
Each in his dearest tongue, his neighbor's voice
Though separate by half the globe."

On the map at the left is traced in black lines a long distance circuit extending from Havana, Cuba, across to Florida and thence up along the Atlantic coast to New York, west to Chicago and farther west to San Francisco. We have deployed along that line tonight some men, who are there to talk to us and carry out any orders that we care to give them.

There will be a light shown from time to time indicating the progress of the call. Now, in order to see whether all of our orders have been obeyed and that the men are all at their stations, I will call the roll. I will begin at Havana.

HAVANA: This is Havana, Cuba, Mr. Caldwell talking.

GENERAL CARTY: Mr. Caldwell, do you hear me well to-night?

HAVANA: I hear you very well.

GENERAL CARTY: Well, I hear you very well too. I will go on to Key West. Key West.

KEY WEST: This is Key West, Florida, Mr. Simpson talking.

GENERAL CARTY: Palm Beach.

PALM BEACH: This is Palm Beach, Florida, Mr. Cody talking.

GENERAL CARTY: Jacksonville.

JACKSONVILLE: This is Jacksonville, Florida, Mr. Miller talking.

GENERAL CARTY: Denmark, South Carolina.

DENMARK: This is Denmark, South Carolina, Mr. Rose talking.

GENERAL CARTY: Selma, North Carolina.

SELMA: This is Selma, North Carolina, Mr. Crawford talking.

GENERAL CARTY: Richmond, Virginia.

RICHMOND: This is Richmond, Virginia, Mr. Albert talking.

GENERAL CARTY: We have gotten some distance away from Havana. Richmond, how far are you from Havana?

RICHMOND: One thousand, three hundred and three miles.

GENERAL CARTY: One thousand, three hundred and three miles from Havana?

RICHMOND: Yes, Mr. Carty.

GENERAL CARTY: We will go on. Philadelphia.

PHILADELPHIA: This is Philadelphia, Pennsylvania, Mr. Campbell talking.

GENERAL CARTY: New York.

NEW YORK: This is New York City, Mr. Hawkins talking.

GENERAL CARTY: How far are you from Havana, New York?

NEW YORK: We are one thousand, seven hundred and five miles from Havana.

GENERAL CARTY: What is the weather in New York tonight?

NEW YORK: Clear, calm, temperature about 32 degrees; a little snow on the ground, about six inches.

GENERAL CARTY: A little snow? You call six inches a little snow?

NEW YORK: Yes, sir.

GENERAL CARTY: In some places they call that a blizzard. That would not be good publicity though, would it?

NEW YORK: No, sir.

GENERAL CARTY: Now, we will go on. Harrisburg.

HARRISBURG: This is Harrisburg, Pennsylvania, Mr. Palmer talking.

GENERAL CARTY: Pittsburgh.

PITTSBURGH: This is Pittsburgh, Pennsylvania, Mr. Hamill talking.

GENERAL CARTY: Beaver Dam, Ohio.

BEAVER DAM: This is Beaver Dam, Ohio, Mr. Struble talking.

GENERAL CARTY: How far are you from Havana?

BEAVER DAM: Two thousand, three hundred and forty-one miles.

GENERAL CARTY: Well, we are moving on rapidly. I think I will have to answer from Chicago myself. We are just about the middle of this line. We are right in the middle of things out here.

Now we will go west of Chicago. Davenport, Iowa.

DAVENPORT: This is Davenport, Iowa, Mr. Small talking.

GENERAL CARTY: Omaha.

OMAHA: This is Omaha, Nebraska, Mr. Barker talking.

GENERAL CARTY: North Platte.

NORTH PLATTE: This is North Platte, Nebraska, Mr. Leonard talking.

GENERAL CARTY: Denver.

DENVER: This is Denver, Colorado, Mr. Carr talking.

GENERAL CARTY: And how far are you from Havana?

DENVER: Three thousand, seven hundred and eight miles from Havana.

GENERAL CARTY: What kind of weather have you got in Denver today?

DENVER: The weather is cloudy, about 36 degrees. It has been raining here all day. It is all right now, however.

GENERAL CARTY: It has cleared up now?

DENVER: Yes.

GENERAL CARTY: What is the elevation of Denver?

DENVER: One mile above sea level.

GENERAL CARTY: Still the same old mile, is it? I forgot to ask Havana what the weather is there. It is not snowing today in Havana, is it, Mr. Caldwell?

HAVANA: No, in Havana it is fair.

GENERAL CARTY: Fair?

HAVANA: Temperature 82 degrees.

GENERAL CARTY: It is not raining there, is it?

HAVANA: No, it is fair and clear.

GENERAL CARTY: While it is not raining there, yet we have an idea that Havana is wet, nevertheless.

HAVANA: Your idea is well founded.

GENERAL CARTY: I will tell you something about this that is rather paradoxical. We ought to have Chesterton here to deal with this paradox. It is raining here in Chicago and yet there is a good deal of evidence at this banquet that it is dry. How do you account for that?

HAVANA: I should say you were rather unfortunate.

GENERAL CARTY: Well, we may amend that situation some time.

Now we are going on west here. Rawlins, Wyoming.

RAWLINS: This is Rawlins, Wyoming, Mr. Pinckney talking.

GENERAL CARTY: What is the weather down there?

RAWLINS: Cloudy and dark, about 30 degrees.

GENERAL CARTY: Salt Lake City.

SALT LAKE CITY: This is Salt Lake City, Utah, Mr. Haford talking.

GENERAL CARTY: How far are you from Havana?

SALT LAKE CITY: Four thousand, two hundred and ninety miles from Havana.

GENERAL CARTY: We are getting farther away. Now we will go on to Nevada. Winnemucca.

WINNEMUCCA: This is Winnemucca, Nevada, Mr. Reynolds talking.

GENERAL CARTY: How far are you from Havana?

WINNEMUCCA: Four thousand, six hundred and seven miles.

GENERAL CARTY: Are you having good weather there today?

WINNEMUCCA: We are having very nice weather. The temperature now is about 26 degrees above.

GENERAL CARTY: Have you got any snow?

WINNEMUCCA: We have no snow on the ground, except in the mountains.

GENERAL CARTY: Yes, you can see it. Now we are getting down where it is warmer. Sacramento.

SACRAMENTO: This is Sacramento, California, Mr. Benton talking.

GENERAL CARTY: What is the weather there today?

SACRAMENTO: There is a strong north wind blowing. The temperature is around 48. We had quite a storm last night.

GENERAL CARTY: Are the fruit trees in bloom there?

SACRAMENTO: What is that, General?

GENERAL CARTY: I say, are the trees in bloom now?

SACRAMENTO: Yes, everything is green out here, Mr. Carty.

GENERAL CARTY: That is what I expected. When you get down past Sacramento you get into the verdure. Now we will go on to San Francisco.

SAN FRANCISCO: This is San Francisco, Mr. Bates talking.

GENERAL CARTY: I would recognize your voice, Mr. Bates, wherever you talked.

SAN FRANCISCO: Thank you, Mr. Carty. I recognize yours too.

GENERAL CARTY: I suppose you have the same temperature there as you always do at San Francisco?

SAN FRANCISCO: Well, we are sitting pretty.

GENERAL CARTY: By the way, how cold or warm is it?

SAN FRANCISCO: The temperature is about 59.

GENERAL CARTY: Fifty-nine?

SAN FRANCISCO: I should say it was warming up a little.

GENERAL CARTY: Mr. Bates, I wonder if you could just stand by there for a moment, will you?

SAN FRANCISCO: I will, Mr. Carty.

GENERAL CARTY: And I am going to ask Mr. Caldwell to talk with you later on, but just now I am going to ask Mr. Caldwell if he could not let us have a little music, say a chime of bells or something down there in Havana. Can you do that, Mr. Caldwell?

HAVANA: We will play "Home, Sweet Home" on the chimes for you.

GENERAL CARTY: All right. That ought to be rather affecting for you.

HAVANA: Well, I would like to see my home, sir.

GENERAL CARTY: All right, you will see it one of these days.

HAVANA: Just one moment.

GENERAL CARTY: I thank you.

(The audience then heard the chimes play "Home, Sweet Home" in Havana.)

GENERAL CARTY: Mr. Caldwell.

HAVANA: Yes, sir, Mr. Carty.

GENERAL CARTY: That comes very well indeed. We are very much obliged to you. Now we are going to ask San Francisco for a little music and then afterwards I would like to have our friends here listen to San Francisco and Havana debating any topic that you gentlemen want to select, and we will try to decide fairly on the merits. But before we have the debate, could you give us some music, Mr. Bates, there?

SAN FRANCISCO: Mr. Carty.

GENERAL CARTY: Yes.

SAN FRANCISCO: We are planning to give you a violin solo and also a cornet solo.

GENERAL CARTY: Supposing we try the violin solo first.

SAN FRANCISCO: Violin solo. Miss Price playing "Traumerei."

GENERAL CARTY: That will be very nice.

(The audience then heard "Traumerei" played by violin from San Francisco.)

GENERAL CARTY: Mr. Bates.

SAN FRANCISCO: Yes, sir, Mr. Carty.

GENERAL CARTY: I think we would like to hear that cornet solo.

SAN FRANCISCO: All right, sir.

GENERAL CARTY: That was very fine. Tell the lady that that came through very beautifully.

SAN FRANCISCO: We will ask Mr. Wing to play "Auld Lang Syne."

GENERAL CARTY: That will sound very good.

(A cornet solo of "Auld Lang Syne" was then heard from San Francisco.)

GENERAL CARTY: That was very well received, Mr. Bates.

SAN FRANCISCO: Thank you, sir.

GENERAL CARTY: It has occurred to me since we have been talking that some time or other for the benefit of the Commercial Club we might have a transcontinental minstrel show. You could be one end man, San Francisco, and Havana could be the other end man.

SAN FRANCISCO: You would be the middle man.

GENERAL CARTY: Oh, I would, would I?

SAN FRANCISCO: You know the middle man has to carry the load.

GENERAL CARTY: Well, we have got quite a lot of middle men here.

SAN FRANCISCO: Well, you have my vote.

GENERAL CARTY: You say they use their Bible.

SAN FRANCISCO: What?

GENERAL CARTY: You say they use their Bible?

SAN FRANCISCO: No, I say you have my vote for middle man.

GENERAL CARTY: Oh, I see. Now, Mr. Bates, we would like to have that discussion between you and Mr. Caldwell. You have not finished it, you know. You were having an argument the last time I was on the line.

SAN FRANCISCO: Hello, Mr. Caldwell.

HAVANA: Hello, Mr. Bates.

SAN FRANCISCO: The argument that we had at Cleveland, I would some time like to have some settlement of that discussion.

HAVANA: I can merely say, Mr. Bates, that we will resume when you take your trip to New York that you have been talking about.

San Francisco: Yes. We will talk about it later then. You heard that roll call and these different places telling about their temperatures. As a matter of fact, you and I are about the only people who are really comfortable tonight.

Havana: Yes, just think of some of those fellows who said the temperature was around 26 degrees.

San Francisco: There is something else I would like to tell you. Chicago is not supposed to hear this. We are talking for the benefit of the Commercial Club in Chicago, you know. I remember the days long ago when Chicago had the highest buildings, the greatest number of miles of boulevard, and so on. I am just wondering what the membership of the Commercial Club is. Out here we have twenty-five hundred members in our commercial club, and I think that is much greater than anything Chicago can set up.

Havana: I can only say, Mr. Bates, that I know you can give them quite a run.

San Francisco: Yes. I might say we have got something else out here that might make Chicago envious. Los Angeles is growing so fast that they have about one hundred and fifty square miles, about nine miles greater than Chicago claims.

General Carty: Now, gentlemen, we have been taking a vote on this and we are going to call it a draw.

San Francisco: All right, sir.

General Carty: Before we go farther, there is one thing, Mr. Bates and Mr. Caldwell, that I did not tell the members of the Club, and while the line is on perhaps you would like to hear about it.

San Francisco: Certainly I would, Mr. Carty.

General Carty: As you know, we talked to London the other night and we talked so well that the question is asked constantly when we are going to have commercial service with London, when can we talk from our homes and offices in Chicago to our friends in London.

San Francisco: Can you tell us when, Mr. Carty?

General Carty: I think so. I think I can tell you something about it. If we had in London an equipment similar to that which we use on the American side, it is safe to say that we could converse with London in just the same manner that we are now conversing with you, and that the members of this Club could have London on as one of the end men.

Our experiments are being conducted exactly in accordance with the schedule. We are measuring the electric conditions at each end of the line, so to speak, measuring the receiving currents and noises, and all the other factors that enter into the engineering of the project, and we find that in the hours of darkness the talking can be done better than in the sunlight. For some reason or other the sunlight seems to have an adverse effect upon the results. While we could probably talk well to London at this moment, at twelve o'clock tomorrow, we would have poor results, if any at all. That is all assuming that this interference of other stations is out of the way. While that is a very serious matter, it is not an impossibility. If we would try to talk to London tonight the chances are we would hear as we did in our experiments.

The French in the Ruhr, the Germans at Berlin, the Italian military maneuvers in Italy, stations in Norway are also constantly interfering. We happened to choose for our experiment an hour when we arranged to have things quiet. So we are a long ways from commercial service because of the unreliability of the situation, the undeveloped nature of it. So when commercial service can be established, can be determined only after these measurements are made and long engineering studies conducted. Then we will have the problem of the short business day that is common to London and Chicago, the difficulty of talking at all in the day time, and a lot of difficult questions of that sort; all of those have got to be studied and worked out, and until they are we cannot say anything more definite than what I have now said.

SAN FRANCISCO: That is certainly interesting to us, Mr. Carty.

GENERAL CARTY: I might tell these people here that the first and only commercial wireless telephone circuit that I know of in the world is between Catalina Island and Los Angeles.

SAN FRANCISCO: That is right.

GENERAL CARTY: That service was put in because it was not possible to get a cable in time, so the radio was put in. You will notice on that map that there is a black line that I had hoped we would not have to use tonight, the lower line. That is an emergency circuit. They were just intimating they might have to talk on that. But now I understand we won't have to talk over it.

I was referring to this radio link from Catalina to Los Angeles that was put in because they could not get the cable in time. The cable is now being made in Hawthorne here in Chicago, to be laid there, because it is more dependable. It will carry more traffic per dollar invested by far than the radio, and when that cable is laid we will have the radio there for experimental purposes.

Now, Mr. Bates, I think we will thank you for that discussion with Mr. Caldwell, and I think I will give the good-night roll call, and after that when I come to you I will ask for some final things for you to do for us.

SAN FRANCISCO: All right, sir. I shall be ready.

GENERAL CARTY: Now I will say "good night" to all of these stations. I first want to thank all the men. I forgot to say we have got to thank now a new set of men. Something probably happened. A line five thousand miles long is subject to vicissitudes. We have our men deployed throughout that distance so they are ready to do what men can do to substitute a section when anything goes wrong.

Somewhere on the line, I don't know where, these men are working. Now they tell me it has been righted. I don't know where it was that went wrong.

I will go on with the roll call. I will begin where I began originally.

Good night, Havana.

HAVANA: This is Havana, Cuba. Good night, Chicago.

GENERAL CARTY: Good night, Key West.

KEY WEST: This is Key West, Florida. Good night, Chicago.

GENERAL CARTY: Good night, Palm Beach.

PALM BEACH: This is Palm Beach. Good night, Chicago.

GENERAL CARTY: Good night, Jacksonville.

JACKSONVILLE: This is Jacksonville, Florida. Good night, Chicago.

GENERAL CARTY: Good night, Denmark.

DENMARK: This is Denmark, South Carolina. Good night, Chicago.

GENERAL CARTY: Good night, Selma, North Carolina.

SELMA: This is Selma, North Carolina. Good night, Chicago.

GENERAL CARTY: Good night, Richmond, Virginia.

RICHMOND: This is Richmond, Virginia. Good night, Chicago.

GENERAL CARTY: Good night, Philadelphia, Pennsylvania.

PHILADELPHIA: This is Philadelphia, Pennsylvania. Good night, Chicago.

GENERAL CARTY: Good night, New York City.

NEW YORK CITY: This is New York City. Good night, Chicago.

GENERAL CARTY: Good night, Harrisburg, Pennsylvania.

HARRISBURG: This is Harrisburg, Pennsylvania. Good night, Chicago.

General Carty: Good night, Pittsburgh, Pennsylvania.

Pittsburgh: This is Pittsburgh, Pennsylvania. Good night, Chicago.

General Carty: Good night, Beaver Dam, Ohio.

Beaver Dam: This is Beaver Dam, Ohio. Good night, Chicago.

General Carty: Good night, Davenport. I am skipping Chicago because I am here and I don't want to say good night yet to you folks. Davenport has evidently gone to sleep. They had a temporary break somewhere there, and they were switching from one line to the other. We can be sure there are some busy people somewhere around there.

Davenport: This is Davenport, Iowa. Good night, Chicago.

General Carty: Good night, Omaha, Nebraska.

Omaha: This is Omaha, Nebraska. Good night, Chicago.

General Carty: Good night, North Platte, Nebraska.

North Platte: This is North Platte, Nebraska. Good night, Chicago.

General Carty: Good night, Denver, Colorado.

Denver: This is Denver, Colorado. Good night, Chicago.

General Carty: Good night, Rawlins, Wyoming.

Rawlins: This is Rawlins, Wyoming. Good night, Chicago.

General Carty: Good night, Salt Lake City, Utah.

Salt Lake City: This is Salt Lake City, Utah. Good night, Chicago.

General Carty: Good night, Winnemucca, Nevada.

Winnemucca: This is Winnemucca, Nevada. Good night, Chicago.

General Carty: Good night, Sacramento, California.

Sacramento: This is Sacramento, California. Good night, Chicago.

General Carty: Well, we won't say "good night" finally to San Francisco.

San Francisco: Thank you.

General Carty: Because we know from experience out there how futile that would be.

San Francisco: We don't like to say "good night."

General Carty: Now, Mr. Bates.

San Francisco: Yes, Mr. Carty.

General Carty: As we are going to say "good night" to you I want to thank all of these boys who are on the line still and those associated with them for the very fine work they have done for us tonight. (Applause.)

If you people could understand the skill and the devotion that is involved in doing all of the things that these men have done, you would appreciate the task. Yet they are a very small part of an organization that is at the command of any child, at the command of any sick person in bed who has just strength enough left to lift the telephone and voice enough to speak to command all the services of this army of men who are only a small part of over 260,000 people; and that number is spread out over the map operating two million miles of wire. All that anybody has to do, the humblest person who has a telephone in the house, is just to say a word to any one of those hundreds of thousands or any group of those hundreds of thousands of people, who will immediately set to work to carry out whatever command is given by that person, whoever he might be, in any part of the United States. They will do that work just as well for a child's call as for the greatest man in the country. And these men who are serving us tonight, we never see them, and if they are seen they are merely typical of the tens and hundreds of thousands all over the land. I always like, whenever I can, to show these men that there are some people who know of their work and who appreciate them. (Renewed applause.)

They can all hear that applause, and you may be sure they appreciate it.

SAN FRANCISCO: Yes, we want to thank you for all you have said, Mr. Carty.

GENERAL CARTY: I know they all appreciate it very much and I think you appreciate them.

Now, Mr. Bates, I wonder if we could not have the trumpet sound for us "taps" at San Francisco. Can you do that for us, please?

SAN FRANCISCO: Taps?

GENERAL CARTY: Yes.

SAN FRANCISCO: Yes.

GENERAL CARTY: And after we have heard "taps" that will be the end of my very prolonged talk in many ways. Then Mr. Sunny wishes to make an announcement. We will now hear on the trumpet "taps" in San Francisco.

(The bugle in San Francisco played "taps.")

PRESIDENT SUNNY: I have just received the following telegram from Mr. Samuel Insull, who is in New York:

"Please convey to Brigadier General John J. Carty my extreme regret at my being unable to participate in what I know will be one of the most interesting occasions the members of the Commercial Club have ever enjoyed."

Mr. Insull's forecast was exactly right. This has been one of the most interesting occasions in the history of the Commercial Club. I speak for you all, I know, when I extend to General Carty and his associates and his assistants our very profound and sincere thanks for a very entertaining, enlightening and delightful evening.

TWO HUNDRED AND EIGHTY-SEVENTH REGULAR MEETING

Forty-Fifth Annual Meeting

At the Residence of President B. E. Sunny

4913 Kimbark Avenue

Friday, April 13, 1923.

Closed Meeting: President Sunny Presiding

PROGRAM

Presentation of Reports

Report of Secretary.
Report of Treasurer.
Report of Committee on Plan of Chicago.
Report of Chicago Plan Commission.
Report of Committee on American Merchant Marine.
Report of Committee on Community Chest.
Report of Committee on Educational Institutions.
Proposed Changes in By-Laws.
Annual Election.

President Sunny: Gentlemen, I feel very grateful to you tonight for coming out here in such unusually large numbers.

We are without a secretary tonight on account of the absence of Mr. Cudahy, who could not be present because of sickness in his family. We are on notice by the Nominating Committee that Mr. George E. Scott has been nominated for secretary for the new year, and I think it is only fair that we have a sample of the kind of work he can do before we are asked to vote for him. Will somebody nominate Mr. Scott for secretary?

MR. HAROLD F. McCORMICK: I would like to have the honor of nominating Mr. Scott for secretary.

MR. CARPENTER: I second the motion.

(On a viva voce vote the motion was unanimously carried.)

PRESIDENT SUNNY: The next business is to act on the nomination of the Executive Committee of Mr. W. R. Abbott to membership in this Club to fill a vacancy. I will ask Mr. Thomas E. Wilson to speak with reference to Mr. Abbott.

MR. THOMAS E. WILSON: Mr. President and Gentlemen: I am very glad indeed to second the nomination of Mr. Abbott. It has been my privilege and pleasure to observe the work of Mr. Abbott in the community for a great many years. Since 1912 he has been a very active man in connection with the work of the Chicago Association of Commerce. I think since that time he has been on some of the principal committees each year. He has been a member of the Ways and Means Committee, a director and a member of the Executive Committee, a member of the War Council, and a member of the Americanization Committee of the Association.

Mr. Abbott was not simply a member. He was an active worker, conscientious worker in the Association. He was president of the Industrial Club and as a member of a very active committee of the club put over the first State Industrial Wage Loan Association. That association, of course, was responsible for the elimination of the loan shark in the State of Illinois.

Mr. Abbott has been associated with many of the important working committees in the city of Chicago, working in the interest of the community, working in the interest of the Americanization of newcomers and has been a vice-president of the Boy Scouts of America.

I consider it a privilege to be able to stand up here and

second the nomination of such an able fellow, a fellow who has always responded and responded cheerfully, ably and conscientiously to work in the interest of the community. It is a pleasure to me to second his nomination.

PRESIDENT SUNNY: Are there any other remarks? If not, I will appoint Mr. Carpenter and Mr. Pellet as tellers.

(The tellers distributed, collected and counted the ballots, with the following result:)

PRESIDENT SUNNY: Gentlemen, the tellers report there are fifty-one votes, all in favor of Mr. Abbott, and I declare him duly elected.

The next business is the report of officers and committees. The first report is that of the Secretary. I will call on Mr. Scott to read that.

REPORT OF SECRETARY

Your Secretary reports as follows on subjects connected with the administration of his office during the club year 1922–1923:

The following changes in membership have been recorded:

From Active to Associate:

Hugh J. McBirney, December 8, 1922

Elected to Associate membership:

James A. Patten, December 8, 1922

Resigned:

Active member, Richard C. Hall, May 16, 1922

Active member, Stanley Field, January 17, 1923

The Active Membership has been increased by the election of the following members:

Chauncey B. Borland, May 17, 1922

Edward L. Ryerson, Jr., November 17, 1922

Brig. Gen. Abel Davis, December 8, 1922

Vacancies: There remain five vacancies in the Active Membership. There have been the following removals from membership through death:

Active: Edmund D. Hulbert, March 30, 1923

Associate: Adolphus C. Bartlett, May 30, 1922

Associate: Rensselaer W. Cox, September 26, 1922

Non-Resident: Charles D. Norton, March 6, 1923.

The following table shows the membership at the end of the last five Club years; with the summary of the changes in the different classes of membership during the present year:

	1918–19	1919–20	1920–21	1921–22	1922-23 Accessions	1922-23 Removals	1922-23 Net Total End of Year
Active	90	89	86	86	3	4	85
Associate	22	21	25	27	2	2	27
Non-Resident	19	19	19	20	0	1	19
Retired	3	2	0	0	0	0	0
	134	131	130	133	5	7	131

ATTENDANCE AT CLUB MEETINGS

	Regular Meeting, May 17, 1922 (44th Annual Closed)	282nd Regular Meeting November 17, 1922	283rd Regular Meeting December 8, 1922	284th Regular Meeting January 13, 1923	285th Regular Meeting February 9, 1923 (Closed)	286th Regular Meeting March 9, 1923	Total all Meetings	Average all Meetings	Total Regular Meetings	Average Regular Meetings
Members—										
Active	36	48	54	54	38	39	269	45	269	45
Associate	5	10	3	8	8	6	40	7	40	7
Non-resident	0	0	0	1	0	0	1	....	1	....
Retired	0	0	0	0	0	0	0	0	0	0
Total	41	58	57	63	46	45	310	52	310	52
Guests—										
Club	....	5	5	14	....	35	59	15	59	15
Members	....	139	79	130	....	254	602	150	602	150
Association of Commerce	....	....	54	....	....	...	....	....	....	....
Total	....	144	138	144	....	289	661	165	661	165
Grand Total	41	202	195	207	46	334	971	217	971	217

Average attendance, closed meetings, 44; at open meetings, 235.

Following is a comparison of the regularity of attendance of members at the regular meetings during the Club years 1921–1922 and 1922–1923:

Number of Meetings Attended	1921–1922 April 29, 1921, to April 17, 1922, both inclusive. Regular Meetings			1922–1923 May 17, 1922, to March 9, 1923, both inclusive. Regular Meetings		
	Active	Associate	Non-Resid't	Active	Associate	Non-Resid't
0	5	9	19	5	12	19
1	6	7	0	12	5	1
2	12	8	1	12	6	0
3	20	2	0	27	3	0
4	25	1	0	18	2	0
5	14	1	0	10	0	0
6	7	0	0	5	1	0
Total attendance	302	38	2	269	40	1
Average	50	6	..	45	7	..

Mr. Hugh J. McBirney attended two meetings as an Active member before being transferred to Associate Membership.

Executive Committee Meetings

1922–1923

	May 22	May 31	June 7	June 21	June 27	July 5	July 12	July 19	September 20	September 27	October 11	October 18	November 8	November 15	November 22	November 29	December 13	January 17	January 31	March 14
S. L. Avery	1	1	1	1	1				1	1	1	1			1	1	1			1
J. M. Cudahy	1	1	1	1	1		1	1	1	1		1	1	1		1	1			
S. M. Felton	1		1	1	1	1				1	1		1		1		1	1	1	
V. F. Lawson																			1	1
D. R. McLennan	1	1				1	1	1		1	1		1	1				1		
J. E. Otis			1	1					1	1		1					1	1		1
G. E. Scott		1	1			1	1	1	1			1	1	1	1	1		1	1	1
J. W. Scott	1			1	1	1		1		1	1	1	1	1	1	1	1	1	1	1
B. E. Sunny	1	1	1	1	1	1	1	1	1	1	1	1	1	1	1	1	1	1	1	1
T. E. Wilson		1			1	1		1		1				1						
Total	6	6	6	6	6	6	4	6	5	8	5	6	6	6	5	5	6	6	5	6

EXECUTIVE COMMITTEE MEETINGS

Since taking office the Executive Committee has held twenty meetings, with an average attendance of five out of a membership of ten.

A Year-Book of the usual style is in course of preparation and will be distributed to the members in the near future.

COMMITTEES

In addition to the Executive Committee, the following Standing Committees are now in service:

- Reception Committee
- Committee on Plan of Chicago
- Committee on American Merchant Marine
- Committee on Community Chest
- Committee on Ft. Sheridan and Great Lakes Naval Training Station
- Committee on Revision of the Constitution and Legislation
- Committee on Educational Institutions

PRESIDENT SUNNY: If there are no objections the report of the Secretary will be received and placed on file.

The next business is the report of the Treasurer. In the absence of Mr. Otis, Mr. Walter Wilson will read that report.

REPORT OF TREASURER

Statement of receipts and disbursements for Club Year 1922–1923:

Receipts

From former treasurer (Ezra J. Warner)......	$ 594.03
From members for guests attending dinner....	4,518.50
From members for dues 1922–1923...........	8,475.00
From members, fines for failure to attend meetings..............................	40.00
From sale of "Chicago Plan" book..........	75.00
From assessment for community chest........	11,100.00
From Rand, McNally & Company, royalties on "Education of Citizenship"...........	.36
Overpayment railroad fare entertainment of guests (Hon. J. J. Davis)................	21.38
Interest on bank balance..................	164.21
	$24,988.48

Disbursements

Banquets and meetings.....................	$7,591.45
Outing..................................	388.84
Expenses and entertainment of guests........	203.08
Reporting meetings........................	259.88
Printing and stationery....................	2,157.56
Year-book...............................	857.73
Study financing social agencies..............	7,500.00
R. R. Donnelley & Sons Co., postage, wrapping and delivering "Chicago Plan" and Merchants Club Book..........................	2,615.25

Cablegrams, telegrams and telephone	$ 133.71
Flowers	150.00
Memorials	130.00
Secretary's office expense	1,105.44
Treasurer's office expense	253.50
Insurance, storage and cartage	62.62
Interest on loan	20.63
Paid note, Northern Trust Company	1,500.00
	$24,929.69
Balance (Cash on hand Central Trust Co.)	58.79
	$24,988.48

President Sunny: If there are no objections, the report of the Treasurer will be received and placed on file.

The next report is that of the Chicago Plan Committee. Mr. Busby will present that report. It is, I assure you, a very interesting report, and I know you will all be very glad to hear it.

REPORT OF COMMITTEE ON PLAN OF CHICAGO

MR. BUSBY: As Chairman of the Committee on Plan of Chicago, I beg to submit the following report:

Shortly after our committee was appointed, the Executive Committee of the Club requested us, in view of the high cost of construction and the charges of extravagance and worse made against the city administration, in connection with carrying on public improvements, to confer with Mr. Wacker and his associates on the Chicago Plan Commission, and endeavor to agree upon a schedule for carrying on the work of the Chicago Plan Commission, with the idea of spreading the work and the payment over a number of years, and holding the tax burdens within the taxpayers' ability to pay.

A joint meeting of the Chicago Plan Committee and the Executive Committee of the Commercial Club was held on November 29, 1922, at the Mid-day Club. At this meeting figures were presented and discussed regarding the increase in tax rates from 1915 to 1922, the various city bond issues outstanding, including bond issues for carrying on the Chicago Plan, and considerable other data bearing on the cost of these improvements.

From the data submitted, it appeared that during the period from January 1, 1915, to November 28, 1922, the following bond issues had been authorized by the city of Chicago and other local governmental bodies within Cook County:

City of Chicago............	$76,702,200
Sanitary District of Chicago..	25,000,000
Forest Preserve District of Cook County.............	15,000,000

Cook County	$ 10,600,000
South Park Commissioners	9,220,000
Lincoln Park Commissioners	2,250,000
West Chicago Park Commissioners	1,000,000
	$138,772,200

It also appeared that the tax rates in the city of Chicago, from 1914 to 1921, inclusive, increased 66 per cent, as shown by the following yearly rates:

TAX RATES FOR CITY OF CHICAGO

Year	Towns North	Towns West	Towns South
1914	$5.47	$5.50	$5.15
1915	5.91	5.92	5.61
1916	6.48	6.39	6.10
1917	6.50	6.58	6.15
1918	6.21	6.24	5.85
1919*	5.41	5.36	5.14
1920*	5.89	5.57	5.39
1921*	7.87	7.64	7.38
Actual increase 1914–1921	68%	62%	67%

*Tax rate was levied on one-half assessed valuation, instead of one-third, the previous ratio.

It also appeared from the Tenth Annual Report of the Chicago Plan Commission that approximately $61,500,000 of bonds had been voted for improvement made under the Chicago Plan, in addition to the special assessments levied in aid of these improvements.

After a general discussion as to whether the improvements now being made in furtherance of the Chicago Plan should be accelerated or retarded, it was resolved that a joint meeting of the Chicago Plan Committee of the Commercial Club and the Executive Committee of the Chicago Plan Commission be held for the purpose of discussing the improvements now under way, and future improvements, under the Chicago Plan.

After several efforts to select a convenient date, a joint meeting of the Chicago Plan Committee of the Commercial Club and the Executive Committee of the Chicago Plan Commission was held at the Hotel Sherman, March 16, 1923.

The question discussed was whether the rate of progress in carrying out the Chicago Plan improvements was adding unreasonably to the constantly increasing burdens of taxation. There was a general discussion, which lasted for nearly three hours. Accurate figures, however, were not available. Your Committee suggested that the best thing to do would be to get the facts. This met the approval of all those present, and it was agreed that Mr. Wacker, as Chairman of the Chicago Plan Commission, would prepare and furnish us:

1. A statement showing the bond issues, special assessments and total estimated cost of the ten major Chicago Plan improvements; and

2. The increase in tax rates, due to interest and sinking fund provisions for the bond issues for carrying out the Chicago Plan improvements during the period 1913 to 1923, inclusive.

Attached to this report is a copy of these two very interesting statements.

From these statements it appears that for the ten major Chicago Plan improvements, namely: First, Michigan Avenue; second, Roosevelt Road; third, South Water Street; fourth, Twenty-Second Street; fifth, Ogden Avenue; sixth, Western Avenue; seventh, Ashland Avenue; eighth, Robey Street; ninth, West Side Warehouse District (Polk, Taylor, Clinton, Jefferson and Desplaines streets), and tenth, Indiana Avenue, the total bond issues,—original and additional—amounted to $62,100,000. Estimated total special assessments amounted to $44,426,000, indicating a total cost for these improvements of $106,526,000.

The statement with reference to the increase in tax rates, due to Chicago Plan improvements, shows that in 1913, the percentage of our total tax rate, due to such improvements, amounted to .43 of one per cent; there was a gradual increase up to 1919, when the percentage of the total tax rate rose to 1.18 per cent; in 1920, however, the percentage of our tax rate, due to Chicago Plan improvements, rose to 5.22 per cent, but this percentage has since declined rapidly, and for the year 1923,—covering 1922 taxes,—is 2.4 per cent of the total tax rate, or 19 cents for each $100 of assessed valuation, which is estimated to be one-half of the full value.

Mr. Wacker in his letter of April 11, 1923, transmitting these figures to your Committee, says:

"As the city has reached its limit of indebtedness it can issue new bonds only as outstanding bonds are paid off, which is being done at the rate of about five or six million dollars a year. Hence the real increase cannot possibly be very much greater than it is for the outstanding bonds, which amount is 19 cents per $100 this year and which will decrease proportionately as the bonds are retired.

"The figures in these tables are accurate, having been taken from the official records of the city supplied by the Comptroller's Office. The estimates of the cost to complete the improvements were made by the technical staff of the Board of Local Improvements, and several of these estimates have been checked back by our engineer and found to be correct—such as South Water Street, La Salle Street, Michigan Avenue, Roosevelt Road, and Ogden Avenue."

The foregoing figures show that the increase in general tax rates, due to the bonds issued for Chicago Plan improvements, is not in itself burdensome. These figures do not show the burden to the individual property owner of the special assessments levied in connection with these improvements. The theory of a special assessment is that the property is benefited, at least, to the full amount of the assessment. It is evident that in some cases hardships may fall on the property owners as a result of these special assessments, but taking into account the great majority of property owners, there can be little doubt that the increase in the value of the property assessed has far exceeded the amount of the assessment.

The Chicago Plan Commission also transmitted to your Committee a copy of its Thirteenth Annual Report, covering the year 1922, which we suggest be presented to the Club by Mr. Wacker, chairman of the Commission.

There is one other matter to which we wish to call the Club's attention: Mr. Angus Hibbard requested an opportunity to present to the Chicago Plan Committee of the Club his ideas for the use of the Chicago River for traffic purposes by bridging the river over. A meeting of the Chicago Plan Committee of the Club was held March 23, 1923, at which Mr. Hibbard presented his ideas, and submitted sketches and data concerning his proposed plan.

Mr. James O. Heyworth was present and mentioned a similar plan, originally formulated by him in a letter to Mr. Edgar A. Bancroft, dated November 17, 1919. Both plans agree on the use of the Chicago River for traffic purposes by bridging the river over, the main difference in the two plans being that Mr. Hibbard proposes to bridge the river over at one level, about four feet above the present water level, thus forming a wide boulevard, extending from the intersection of Michigan Avenue and the river west to the junction of the north and south branches, thence north in the north branch of the river to Ogden Avenue, and south in the south branch of the river to 12th Street. This boulevard would pass under existing bridges, and a portion of the boulevard space in the center would be used for a public garage.

Mr. Heyworth's plan provides for two levels, one about six feet above the present level of the river, which is left to be used for freight traffic, containing a number of tracks for transportation of freight cars, drawn by electric locomotives, with suitable connections to existing railroad terminals and a second level on practically the same level as existing bridges. This second, or upper level, would be used for boulevard traffic, the same as Michigan Boulevard.

This proposed improvement of the river is based on the proposition that river traffic has steadily decreased during the past decade; that lighterage has become uneconomical, and that the value of the river for purposes of navigation has become negligible, and is offered in lieu of the pending two-level South Water Street improvement, which is designed to connect with the upper and lower surfaces of Michigan Avenue at both river and South Water Street. The upper level will connect with the north and south streets bridging the main channel of the river, and the bridges at La Salle Street and Wabash Avenue when completed, and will give the city two greatly needed new east and west streets through one of the most congested areas in the downtown district.

As a result of the discussion, it was agreed that Mr. Heyworth and Mr. Hibbard would prepare for the information of the Club a summary of their plans, and that this summary together with all other drawings, and data, furnished by Mr. Heyworth and Mr. Hibbard, be transmitted to the Executive Committee of the Club for such action as that Committee deemed advisable. These papers are transmitted herewith.

Respectfully submitted,

LEONARD A. BUSBY.

Chairman, Chicago Plan Committee the Commercial Club.

The report of the Chicago Plan Commission is submitted, Mr. Chairman, for Mr. Wacker's presentation to the Club.

THIRTEENTH ANNUAL REPORT OF THE CHICAGO PLAN COMMISSION

For the Year 1922

Mr. Wacker: Gentlemen: During 1922 the Chicago Plan Commission, its executive officers, and its technical staff, continued their efforts toward the carrying forward of pending improvements rather than the inauguration of new projects. It is believed that this should continue to be the policy of the Plan Commission during 1923.

Progress on the Plan of Chicago during 1922 is recorded as follows:

Ashland Avenue: Ordinance passed by the City Council, June 21, 1922, for opening and extending Ashland Avenue from West 95th Street to Beverly Avenue.

Permission was granted by the Federal Government for a bridge at Ashland Avenue across the north branch of the Chicago River.

The ordinance for widening Ashland Avenue between Pratt Boulevard and Devon Avenue was recommitted by the City Council to the Board of Local Improvements. All other sections of the Ashland Avenue improvement are on trial in the County Court.

Bridges: Our technical staff has continued to assist the city in developing the design and the architectural work,—including operators' houses, lighting standards, etc.,—of all bridges under construction.

Clinton Street: Condemnation suit on trial in County Court.

Desplaines Street: Condemnation suit on trial in County Court.

Forest Preserves: During 1922, 3,281.41 acres of

forest preserves were acquired, bringing the present total up to 24,797.85 acres, obtained at a total cost of $11,817,889.26.

In the course of the year 6,083,000 persons visited the forest preserves.

Ground was broken for the new Zoological Gardens in the forest preserves near Riverside, on October 27, 1922. At this time Chairman Charles H. Wacker made an address, of which one thousand copies were subsequently printed and distributed by the Cook County Board of Forest Preserve Commissioners.

GOOD ROADS: The Cook County Board laid forty-seven miles of roads during 1922, at a total cost of approximately $1,410,000.

HARBORS: Colonel Curtis M. Townsend, U. S. A., was appointed on January 25, 1922, federal member of the Interstate Harbor Commission of Illinois and Indiana, the Commission which is empowered to create and operate the proposed Illiana Harbor.

Federal permission for the proposed Lake Calumet industrial harbor was granted in December, 1922, and it is expected that the harbor will be in operation by 1930.

Several projects studied by the Plan Commission and incorporated in the "Revised Map of the City of Chicago and the County of Cook" have a bearing on this project, as they will provide street circulation through and surrounding the area involved in the harbor districts; they are 103rd Street, Stony Island Avenue, Cottage Grove Avenue, 130th Street, 134th Street, and Torrence Avenue.

INDIANA AVENUE: Ordinance passed by City Council December 14, 1921, for widening Indiana Avenue to 100 feet between 16th Street and 22nd Street. The assessment roll is about ready to file in court.

JEFFERSON STREET: Condemnation suit on trial in County Court.

LAKE FRONT: The filling in between 16th and 23rd

streets is making rapid progress under the direction of the South Park Commissioners.

The grading plans for Grant Park north of Roosevelt Road were completed during the summer, and the work is now well advanced. Plans for the architectural development of the park east of the Illinois Central tracks, in extension of the work done north of the Art Institute, have been ordered by the South Park Commissioners.

LA SALLE STREET: Widening between Washington Street and Lincoln Park approved by the Plan Commission November 28, 1922, and a resolution to that effect immediately forwarded to his honor, the Mayor, and the City Council.

LINCOLN PARK: The Executive Committee of the Plan Commission on January 11, 1922, approved the plan agreed upon between Consultant E. H. Bennett, and the engineer of the Lincoln Park Board, for the treatment of Lake Shore Drive between Oak Street and North Avenue.

MAJOR STREET SYSTEM: Preliminary plans have been prepared for a traffic regulation system providing separate "through streets" for rapid traffic. It is hoped that this plan may be ready to submit to the Commission some time this year.

MARKET STREET: Ordinance for widening between Lake and Randolph streets to permit of lower level entrance to South Water Street, passed by City Council on January 25, 1922.

MICHIGAN AVENUE: Completed.

Designs for the embellishment of the bridge houses were agreed upon and the contracts let for the four groups of statuary proposed.

The four groups of sculpture were designed as follows:

Northwest pylon: "The Discoverers."

Northeast pylon: "The Pioneers."

Southwest pylon: "Defense" or "Fort Dearborn."

Southeast pylon: "Regeneration—The Chicago Fire."

The two north groups have been assigned to Mr. Earle Fraser and the two south groups to Mr. Henry Hering.

OGDEN AVENUE: Construction work began April 8, 1922, on the northeastern section between Clark Street and Division and Halsted streets. This section is now complete.

Buildings are now being torn down on the southwestern section between Randolph Street and Chicago Avenue.

No work has as yet been undertaken on the central portion between Chicago Avenue and Division Street.

In accordance with our usual practice, attention has been given by the staff of consultants to the design of the viaducts and the bridges involved.

PAGEANT OF PROGRESS: At the 1922 Pageant of Progress the Board of Local Improvements distributed 100,000 copies of a booklet entitled, "The Chicago Plan," describing the various Chicago Plan improvements now going forward; and also exhibited a large scale model of the South Water Street improvement.

PERSHING ROAD: Remains in statu quo.

POLK STREET: Condemnation suit on trial in County Court.

POST OFFICE: The matter of providing really adequate postal facilities, worthy of a city of the first class, made little headway during 1922. The Chicago Plan Commission has so often described what the new main post office must be, and the advantages of having it located upon the two-block Canal Street site between the North Western and the new Union Station terminals, that it is not necessary to repeat these points here.

At the meeting of the Commission on May 26, 1922, a resolution embodying the position of the Commission in the post office matter and calling for action was adopted and sent to the Mayor, the City Council, the Railway Terminal Commission, Illinois Senators and Representatives, and Post Officials in Chicago and Washington.

PRAIRIE AVENUE: Widening between 16th and 23rd streets recommended by the Plan Commission May 26, 1922, and a resolution to that effect immediately forwarded to his honor, the Mayor, and the City Council.

RAILWAY TERMINALS: Good preliminary progress was made on the electrification plans of the Illinois Central, and construction work continued on the West Side Union Station foundations.

There has been an occasional review of the terminal situation by our consultants and the Railway Terminal Commission, and also of various details which have arisen in connection with the execution of the two big projects: the Illinois Central and the Union stations.

RANDOLPH STREET: Condemnation suit ended February 18, 1922. The date for the start of construction is still undetermined.

RIVER STRAIGHTENING: The question of straightening the river is involved with the rearrangement of the terminal facilities of the railroads occupying the territory south of the loop district. These railroads are composed of three groups; namely, the Grand Central group; the La Salle Street group; and the Dearborn group.

The Railway Terminal Commission reports that each of these groups is now actively at work with special staffs on plans for the rearrangement of terminal facilities predicated upon the straightening of the Chicago River. The plans of at least two of these groups are being prepared along lines in harmony with the recommendations of the Chicago Plan and the Railway Terminal Commissions.

While substantial progress is reported on the preparation of these plans, the twelfth annual report for 1921 of the Chicago Plan Commission pointed out that eight years of the fifteen-year period provided in the Union Station ordinance during which the railroads, representing 50 per cent of the ownership of lands abutting on the river, within the limits of the proposed straightening, are obligated to co-operate in river straightening, had expired. It is therefore of the utmost importance that pressure be brought to bear, to the end that the plans referred to above not only be completed as soon as possible, but that an ordinance or ordinances embodying these proposed changes, and providing for the straightening of the river be enacted as speedily as possible.

This is essential, in order that the city may not lose the benefits it secured with reference to river straightening in the Union Station and collateral ordinances, and that the public may no longer be deprived of the privileges and benefits which will accrue to it through the proposed river straightening.

It is now nine years since the passage of the ordinance, and no concrete achievement is to be seen.

ROBEY STREET: Late in 1922 an attempt was made to have the Robey Street improvement abandoned, but, following the recommendation of the Chicago Plan Commission, the order to abandon the improvement was placed on file by the City Council.

ROOSEVELT ROAD: The south half of that viaduct between the river and Wabash Avenue is practically complete, and it is expected that work upon the north half, including the construction of the bridge, will be begun shortly.

SIXTEENTH STREET: Widening between Prairie and Michigan avenues recommended by the Plan Commission on May 26, 1922, and a resolution to that effect immediately forwarded to his honor, the Mayor, and the City Council.

A re-study of this improvement has been made necessary by reason of the fact that the Illinois Central Railroad holdings have been extended to take in the property down to the north line of Sixteenth Street.

SOUTH PARK AVENUE: Condemnation suit on trial in County Court.

SOUTH WATER STREET: On January 11, 1922, the Executive Committee approved the Wabash Avenue connection with the upper level of South Water Street. On May 23, 1922, the Executive Committee approved three new connections between Lake Street and the lower level of South Water Street, and other detail changes in the plan.

On June 21, 1922, the City Council passed ordinances for the three new lower level entrances; and on June 29, 1922, passed the construction ordinance.

The assessment roll was filed in the Circuit Court on June 5, 1922.

Two letters and a pamphlet entitled "South Water Street Facts," explaining that the estimated cost would be $20,000,000 instead of $7,000,000, were sent to every property owner in the assessed district and to every individual or firm doing business on South Water Street. This publicity might not unreasonably have been expected to call forth some objections to the improvement, nevertheless it is a fact that not one single protest was made against the plan or against going ahead with it.

The condemnation trial did not begin during 1922 because the property owners were endeavoring to reach an agreement with the city in the matter of allowing a public benefit.

TAYLOR STREET: Condemnation suit on trial in County Court.

TWENTY-SECOND STREET: Ordinance for widening between Calumet Avenue and Michigan Avenue passed by City Council, January 13, 1922.

Ordinance for widening between Michigan and Archer avenues passed by City Council, April 12, 1922.

The ordinance passed January 13, 1922, included the 120-foot-wide diagonal street between the intersection of 22nd Street and Calumet Avenue and the intersection of South Park Avenue and 23rd Street, and also the widening of 23rd Street between South Park Avenue and the Illinois Central railroad tracks.

In co-operation with the South Park Board and the city authorities, our consultants have studied the details of the arrangement of the plaza formed by the intersection of these streets, its lighting and the safety islands. Plans for the architectural development of the entrance to the viaduct over the tracks are being developed also.

West Side Warehouse District: Five street improvements: Polk, Taylor, Clinton, Jefferson, and Desplaines streets, in the area between Halsted Street, the Chicago River, Harrison Street, and Roosevelt Road, are all on trial in the County Court.

Western Avenue: Some sections of the Western Avenue improvement at the far northern and the far southern ends of the street are under construction, and the remaining sections are on trial in the County Court.

Zoning: The Chicago Zoning Commission practically completed its tentative zoning ordinance during 1922, and set the date of the first public hearing for January 22, 1923.

Throughout the period of study of the zoning plans the co-ordination of Chicago Plan projects with the zoning has been kept in mind, and efforts have been made along this line to the mutual benefit of both departments of work.

The data which the Chicago Plan Commission supplied without cost to the Zoning Commission saved the city an expense of many thousands of dollars.

Thirty-eight Chicago Plan stereopticon lectures were delivered during 1922, to audiences aggregating 12,395 persons.

In addition to these lectures a number of talks were made. Notable among them were addresses by Chairman Wacker at the ceremonies in connection with breaking ground for the new Zoological Gardens; at Decatur, Illinois, before the Illinois Chamber of Commerce, on the subject of "Gaining

Support for a City Planning Movement"; and two Plan talks broadcasted by radio from the City Hall station.

Newspaper publicity has continued undiminished, and the press of Chicago has been most generous and effective in its unremitting and unparalleled support of the Chicago Plan and the work of the Chicago Plan Commission.

The Associated Press sent two Chicago Plan stories to more than 1,300 newspapers, located in every state in the Union, in Alaska, the Hawaiian Islands, the Philippines, in Mexico, Central and South America, and, in a less general way, in all Europe.

Motor News, with a circulation of 35,000, contained three splendid Plan stories in the course of the year.

The extension department of the Art Institute of Chicago held a series of "Better Homes" meetings in five of the Chicago high schools, and one of the lecturers made a fine statement at each meeting concerning the Plan of Chicago.

A textbook entitled "Citizenship," published in New York, included a chapter on city planning which contained Chicago Plan data and pictures.

The Chicago Boosters' Publicity Club used Chicago Plan material in connection with its campaign of publicity.

One thousand copies of a Chicago Plan pamphlet were sent for distribution at the International Exposition of Health and Safety, held in Oakland, California, in November, 1922.

Out of town newspapers containing Chicago Plan stories which have come to our attention, include the *New York Tribune*, the *New York Times*, and the *Dallas* (Texas) *News;* while the *Christian Science Monitor* has run half a dozen good Chicago Plan articles.

Chicago Plan pictures and data were used in a number of magazines and trade publications, among which may be mentioned the *Dearborn Independent*, 600,000 circulation; *Popular Mechanics*, 465,000; *Chicago Commerce*, 6,000;

Aryan Imposcope, 25,000; *Barrel and Box*, 4,500; *M. Born & Company* (trade journal), 250,000; *Judicious Advertising*, two stories; *souvenir book of the American Gymnastic Union*, 25,000; *Blum Building Catalogue*, 3,000; *Forman's Guide*, 60,000; *Theodore A. Koch's Catalogue; S. W. Straus & Company Catalogue; Rand-McNally Souvenir Guide to Chicago; Press Club of Chicago 1922 Reference Book;* and three Chicago Plan pictures were used in 25,000 copies of the Nashville, Chattanooga & St. Louis Railroad tourist folders distributed throughout the South.

Professor George Breed Zug, head of the Department of Fine Arts, Dartmouth College, and Professor H. Miller Scott, of the Ohio State University, were furnished with considerable Chicago Plan data, also pictures and stereopticon slides, to assist them in formulating city planning courses for Dartmouth College and the Ohio State University.

Since the death of Mr. Walter D. Moody in November, 1920, Mr. Eugene S. Taylor, office manager, who has been connected with the Chicago Plan Commission ever since the beginning, has performed his duties in a manner eminently satisfactory to the executive officers and the Commission.

For the past thirteen years the efforts of the Chicago Plan Commission have had the unqualified support and assistance of all governmental authorities—city, county, park, drainage, state, and national; of the press of Chicago; of the Commercial Club; of civic organizations, and of the people at large. Such wide support—unstinted, cordial and effective—given so continuously for so long a period of time, is unique in the annals of American municipal history.

We are truly appreciative—indeed, humbly grateful, for this manifestation of public confidence in our civic endeavors. Our only regret is that it should be impossible to express our deep and sincere gratitude to every one who, during the past thirteen years, has assisted the Chicago Plan Commission in its effort to make Chicago a better place both for business and for residence.

I would like, however, Mr. Chairman, to add a few figures to this statement, with your kind permission. I would like to call the attention of this Club to what is being done in other cities.

Other cities are improving economic and physical conditions in order to make it possible for their merchants and manufacturers to save time and money in the conduct of business, and thereby take away much of the business that now is Chicago's.

The public improvement programs now going forward or proposed in leading American cities—including projects now under way and contemplated—for the opening and widening of streets; the improvement of transportation facilities; and the development of railway terminals, ports, harbors, etc., are as follows, a considerable part of the work already having been completed, other parts being under construction, while still others are proposed for early realization.

Baltimore........	$101,000,000—per capita debt,	$100.54
Boston..........	22,500,000—per capita debt,	107.25
Buffalo..........	20,000,000—per capita debt,	70.58
Cincinnati.......	18,000,000—per capita debt,	190.06
Cleveland........	120,000,000—per capita debt,	95.75
Des Moines......	7,000,000—per capita debt,	53.36
Detroit..........	28,000,000—per capita debt,*	
Kansas City.....	42,000,000—per capita debt,	64.53
Milwaukee.......	23,000,000—per capita debt,	44.53
Minneapolis......	14,500,000—per capita debt,	74.50
New Orleans.....	99,000,000—per capita debt,	109.52
New York.......	880,000,000—per capita debt,	182.93
Philadelphia.....	268,000,000—per capita debt,	81.16
Pittsburgh.......	22,000,000—per capita debt,	107.91
Portland, Ore.....	21,000,000—per capita debt,	82.45

*Not reported.

St. Louis........	103,000,000—per capita debt,	$19.42
St. Paul.........	39,000,000—per capita debt,	40.13
San Francisco....	135,000,000—per capita debt,	96.75

In contrast to this, Chicago's total per capita indebtedness for all purposes, including the corporate school, county, park and Sanitary District bonds, amounts to only $32.31.

Mr. Chairman, let me say just one thing further. There is a report made here, of which I know nothing, in regard to South Water Street. If that is to be taken up and disposed of by the Executive Committee, I shall ask for the Chicago Plan Commission a hearing before any decisive step is taken.

PRESIDENT SUNNY: With regard to this matter I cannot help but recall the general atmosphere which prevailed a year ago, the extremely high cost of all kinds of labor, the unrestrained charges of graft and fraud on the part of the city administration, in expenditures for these improvements and the general alarm that was felt that too much money was being spent, substantially under the auspices of the Commercial Club. Happily that situation has changed. Today, for the first time in your experience and mine, a mayor of Chicago attended a public meeting at the LaSalle Hotel of the soldiers' organization, which meeting was presided over by Mr. Dawes. Mayor Dever was there and he made a statement that warmed all of our hearts with reference to the present and future of Chicago, with respect to its administration, to the honesty of its officials, to the constructive program for work along strict business lines, cutting out the waste. The best testimony of the earnestness of the Mayor in that respect lies in the fact that he has persuaded our fellow member, Colonel Sprague, to be his commissioner of public works. The acceptance of that appointment by Colonel Sprague is a compliment to the Mayor, and it is a compliment to us that that appointment has been made. It is a guarantee that the kind of work that has been indicated by Mr. Busby and by Mr. Wacker in their very interesting reports is going to go forward along honest lines.

In addition to the expenditures that Mr. Busby stated in his report, the South Park Commissioners have been given authority to spend $20,000,000, which is merely the beginning of a program for the extending and improving of the South Park System with reference to the outer boulevards. In a few years from now, if that money has been spent—and it can and will be spent wisely, sanely and with great discretion—we ought to have the most beautiful city there is on God's green footstool. I am sure of that, because there is no other city with the opportunity we have for improvement along both beautification and economic lines. So I feel very much encouraged over the situation. I feel we have made a new and fine start. I feel that all the fraud and crookedness and rottenness is behind us, and that we can forget it.

MR. WACKER: Do I understand, Mr. Chairman, that I will have the privilege of appearing before the Executive Committee on the South Water Street proposition?

PRESIDENT SUNNY: You certainly will, Mr. Wacker.

MR. WACKER: All right, if that is understood.

PRESIDENT SUNNY: Will you discuss Mr. Busby's report and Mr. Wacker's report, or what is your pleasure concerning these reports?

MR. WALTER H. WILSON: I move that they be received with thanks.

MR. RUFUS C. DAWES: I second that motion.

(On a viva voce vote the motion was unanimously carried.)

PRESIDENT SUNNY: The next business is the report of the Merchant Marine Committee, Mr. Heyworth.

REPORT OF COMMITTEE ON MERCHANT MARINE

MR. HEYWORTH: During the year of 1922 the executive officers of our National Government, after the experience of some four years of government ownership and operation of a national merchant marine, urged legislation such as would provide some means by which the large investment in its ships and the annual deficit of some $50,000,000 per year could be retrieved and the annual loss be reduced.

In co-operation with the United States Shipping Board, ship operators, and private ship owners and operators, a bill was drawn and presented to Congress for passage. The United States Ship Subsidy Bill had the approval of the Government administration officers and shipping experts, and was recommended to Congress for immediate favorable action.

The Executive Committee of the Commercial Club of Chicago decided that the bill should receive their consideration and action. To this end Captain William H. Stayton, president of the Baltimore Steamship Company, was invited to address the Club on December 8, 1922. By order of the Executive Committee this speech was ordered printed and circulated, thus receiving the support of the Commercial Club of Chicago.

Through the splendid co-operation of the President, Mr. Sunny, Mr. Samuel M. Felton, and the members of the Committee, the Merchant Marine Committee of the Club arranged for five speeches by Captain Stayton—one at Rockford, Illinois, two in Wisconsin, two in Iowa, and others as far west as Hastings and Grand Island, Nebraska.

Before this work was undertaken there was but little interest in the Middle West, and especially in the Mississippi Valley, although this valley produces 70 per cent of the total exports of the United States.

In the House of Representatives when the bill came to a vote, a majority of all those states which do not touch the Atlantic, Pacific or Gulf voted favorably for the bill, a vote that never before has happened in connection with the merchant marine. In the Senate, had the bill come to a vote, there were enough Senators pledged to pass it. Many of these came from the Central West. However, a practice of "rule or ruin" which our form of government today permits, allowed a few radical Senators, with no moral sense as to the moral right of the majority to be heard, to stop and destroy the proper functioning of our executive body.

On February 9, 1923, the Club endorsed the Ship Subsidy Bill.

The results of the Congressional vote of the Middle West, according to Captain Stayton, something that never before has happened in connection with the merchant marine, indicates that the Club's activity in circulating well advised information and arranging for speeches to put the facts before the public, has succeeded.

From the results herein stated I am convinced that the Commercial Club of Chicago should likewise carry the weight of its opinion and judgment to the people. Furthermore, that its position on all public questions considered should be stated to the public in a way to reach the public and be followed up with the full support and interest of the members of the Club.

At the date of this report it seems that the United States Shipping Board is unable to come to an understanding with ship owners and operators. The continued operation of the United States ships by the Shipping Board means an estimated loss per year of $50,000,000, in addition to which it is thought that the depreciation of the ships will be very great and not met by proper maintenance. Without aid from the Government ship owners and operators do not respond in offering the proper value for the ships, nor, as proposed by the United States Shipping Board, are they willing to agree to keep ships operating in certain lines of travel for a certain number of years. In other words, without compensation and help from the Government, ship owners and operators are not willing to take over the ships unless bought at a very cheap price, at which price the Shipping Board is not willing to sacrifice the ships.

Therefore, if the two parties cannot come to an agreement mutually satisfactory, it seems that the administration must further press the adoption of a ship subsidy bill which in the minds of all interested is satisfactory.

As stated by the Shipping Board, the subsidy required would not exceed $30,000,000 a year for ten years, and if this bill passed, the ships would be taken over at a price which would be much more commensurate with their worth than can be obtained in any other way.

The Commercial Club of Chicago has endorsed the Ship Subsidy Bill. The press the last two weeks has put before the public the status of the negotiations between the Shipping Board and ship owners and operators. In view of these conditions, we recommend that the question be put to the Club whether or not the Club as a body shall further assist the passage of a ship subsidy bill, said assistance to be in manner and means determined by the Executive Committee of the Club.

Respectfully submitted,

JAMES O. HEYWORTH, *Chairman*
Committee on Merchant Marine, Commercial Club of Chicago
FREDERIC W. UPHAM, *Vice-chairman*
H. M. BYLLESBY
EDWARD F. CARRY
ROBERT P. LAMONT

Cyrus H. McCormick
Charles Piez
James Simpson
Robert W. Stewart
H. A. Wheeler

President Sunny: Gentlemen, you have heard the report of the Committee on Merchant Marine. Any suggestions? If not, the report will be received and placed on file.

The next report is that of the Committee on Fort Sheridan and Great Lakes, Mr. John Pirie, Chairman. Mr. Pirie is not able to be here tonight and the Secretary will read his report.

REPORT OF COMMITTEE ON FORT SHERIDAN AND GREAT LAKES NAVAL TRAINING STATION

SECRETARY SCOTT: The Committee on the Fort Sheridan and Great Lakes Naval Training Station beg to report that all legislation and permits required to construct the new highway through the Reservation from the Fort Sheridan Station to the Sacred Heart School have been obtained, and work will proceed when weather permits.

An extensive campaign was carried out by a number of clubs and other organizations to persuade the Navy Department that its definite plan to curtail the activities of the Great Lakes Station was unfair to the Middle West. This campaign was entirely successful, and a reasonable arrangement is now assured, the necessary appropriation having been made.

Respectfully submitted,

JOHN T. PIRIE, *Chairman.*

PRESIDENT SUNNY: You have heard the report of that committee, gentlemen. Are there any suggestions? If not, it will be received and placed on file.

The next report is that of the Committee on Community Chest, Mr. Walter Wilson.

REPORT OF COMMITTEE ON COMMUNITY CHEST

Mr. Walter H. Wilson: Your Committee is not ready to report, because the report is not fully prepared. You will recall this Club made an assessment upon its members of $10,000, to make a survey among the charitable organizations, and report. Under that $11,100 was collected. The first meeting of this endeavor was held the 23rd day of November. At that meeting 160 social agencies were represented. There were also thirty-one agencies controlled by the Catholic charities represented, and eighteen agencies from the Jewish charities. Those agencies were divided into groups. Each group elected two delegates to the conference to act as a committee to make this survey.

I have with me a report of what has been done. It would not be fair to those conducting the survey to read that report tonight, nor to the Club, but I believe it is one of the greatest works that has been done. I would like to offer my compliments to Mr. Willoughby Walling, the chairman of the social agencies, who has been a great help to this Committee and to your Club, and about whom we shall hear further on.

It will take, I believe, two months or perhaps three to complete this report. Then, I think, Mr. President, the Club ought to have a special meeting, or devote some time of some meeting to hear this report, because it will be of very great importance.

President Sunny: If there is no objection, the report of progress by Mr. Wilson will be received and placed on file.

The next report is that of the Educational Committee, Mr. Rufus Dawes.

REPORT OF COMMITTEE ON EDUCATIONAL INSTITUTIONS

MR. RUFUS C. DAWES: Mr. Chairman, I really have no report to submit. I wrote a letter to the Secretary stating that in lieu of a report I would submit the following statement:

In your letter of July 19, 1922, announcing the appointment of this Committee, you quoted as follows from a letter from Mr. Oliver T. Wilson:

"The time is coming, if these universities (Chicago and Northwestern) are to continue in their development, that the burden must more and more come upon the men of means in Chicago and vicinity. In view of this situation does it not seem to you that a committee should be appointed from the Commercial Club, who would study the various institutions of Chicago, and report back to the membership as to the character of work they are doing, the service they are rendering to Chicago, and their plans for future development."

And on behalf of the Executive Committee you stated that an investigation and report was desired "not only of the institutions of higher education, but educational institutions in general."

Appalled by the magnitude of this commission, I immediately called a meeting of the Committee which was attended by all of its members with the exception of Mr. Morton and Mr. Ryerson, who were unavoidably absent. Mr. Wilson at some length explained the motives which actuated this suggestion, stating that it was his chief desire that the members of the Club should be more fully informed about the work that is being done by the institutions of higher education in Illinois, the increasing demands upon them, the obvious necessity for enlarged facilities, and the possible enlargement of the opportunity for the extension of practical education.

It was the sentiment of the Committee that if the Executive Committee regarded the general consideration of the problems of education a matter of practical interest at the present time, it ought to invite the presidents of the Chicago University, the Northwestern University and the Illinois State University, to divide between them the time at one of our regular meetings, and to make addresses upon subjects to be selected by them, but of such a nature as to cover the entire field. This was recommended by the Committee as offering the best opportunity to give to the members of the Club full information upon these important subjects.

The Committee believed that this would be of value to the members of the Club, whether or not the purposes desired by the Executive Committee could be fully attained by such a discussion. The Committee, realizing the indefinite scope of the study which had been submitted to them, asked that the outline of its work should be specifically stated, but have received no further instructions, and have held no further meetings.

PRESIDENT SUNNY: The situation here on the South Side with reference to the University of Chicago is very illustrative of the situation all over the country with regard to educational institutions. Six years ago we had an enrollment here in the University of Chicago of five thousand. Now the enrollment is twelve thousand, and there is no corresponding increase in the housing facilities to take care of such a large enrollment. These figures are duplicated all over the country and I think it is one of the most grave questions we have to deal with.

If there is no objection, the report will be received and placed on file.

The next business is that of the proposed changes in the by-laws recommended by the Executive Committee.

At the closed meeting of the Club in February, it was evident that there was considerable sentiment in favor of increasing the active membership of the Commercial Club from ninety to some larger number, so that at our meetings all through the year we would have a representation that would justify the work of the Executive Committee in bringing men from long distances to address the Club. At some of the meetings during the year, as was pointed out, the attendance was small because of absences, especially the meetings in the early spring of the year.

The Executive Committee has worked out certain changes in the by-laws, which were submitted a month ago, and which we should vote on tonight.

The first amendment is in Section 2, Article I, the substance of which is that the active membership is increased from ninety to one hundred and twenty-five. The proposed amendment to Section 2, Article I, covers two subjects, and I think we ought to vote on them separately. The first proposition we will deal with, therefore, is whether you will approve the proposed change in the number of active members from ninety to one hundred and twenty-five. To get the question before us, will somebody move that we adopt it?

MR. HAROLD F. MCCORMICK: I will make that motion, Mr. Chairman.

MR. WALTER H. WILSON: I second it.

MR. SPRAGUE: I would like to suggest the addition of two words, Mr. President. "Active members are responsible for the varied undertakings of the Club, and will accept"—I would like to move the insertion there of the words "and perform."

MR. WALTER H. WILSON: I will second that motion.

PRESIDENT SUNNY: The motion is on Colonel Sprague's

amendment, to insert the words "and perform" in the proposed amendment as indicated by him.

(On a viva voce vote the motion was unanimously carried.)

PRESIDENT SUNNY: The question is now on the adoption of the amendment, which increases the number of active members from ninety to one hundred and twenty-five.

MR. ROSENWALD: I move the adoption of the amendment, Mr. Chairman.

MR. CHARLES G. DAWES: I second the motion.

(On a viva voce vote the motion was unanimously carried.)

MR. SUNNY: The next amendment strikes out the provision "Active Members upon reaching the age of sixty-five years shall automatically become Associate Members," and substitutes therefore, in Section 3, Article 1, the following:

Any Active Member upon reaching the age of sixty-five years, may at his written request to the Executive Committee, and with the Committee's approval, become an Associate Member.

After extended discussion in which Messrs. Robinson, Walter H. Wilson, Glessner, Donnelley and Baker took part, and on motion of Mr. Baker, the words "and with the Committee's approval" were stricken out and the amendment adopted.

PRESIDENT SUNNY: Gentlemen, the next proposition is that Section 7, Article I, shall be changed so as to read as follows:

"The Secretary shall notify the members whenever a vacancy in the Active Membership occurs.

"It is the duty of members to submit to the Secretary for the information of the Executive Committee names of citizens eligible for membership by reason of their personality, general reputation, and their contributions in effective interest and service to the commonwealth. Each nominee must receive the unanimous vote of the Executive Committee, and thereupon the Secretary will notify the members that the nominee will be voted upon at the next meeting of the Club. Any member who has objection to the nominee must immediately advise a member of the Executive Committee thereof. Two weeks must elapse between the date of notice and the meeting at which the vote is taken. The voting shall be by ballot, and three negative votes shall defer the admission of such nominee. If the names of two or more nominees are printed on the ballot, opportunity will be given to cast a separate vote for each nominee."

I would like to explain that there is very general objection to the present form of ballot, which gives an opportunity to vote for or against, and which points out specifically the possibility of defeating the nominee. It is suggestive and in some cases offensive, and as a matter of practice, we do not count these ballots that come in by mail, so that the form of the ballot can very well be changed and be more satisfactory.

Mr. Lawson suggested at the last meeting an amendment to the section I have just read, the substance of which was, I think, that not more than one name should be suggested unless there were six vacancies.

Mr. Lawson: I cannot state it right now. I do not find it in the paragraphs you mentioned.

President Sunny: Your suggestion we do not find among the papers here. Mr. Cudahy is away. It is probably in his file.

Mr. Lawson: I cannot find that amendment among the ones you have printed here.

President Sunny: We have eighty-five active members now, so there are five vacancies, and with the authority you have given tonight by the change in the first section, there will be forty vacancies to be filled. I think perhaps it would be wise to give the Executive Committee the largest latitude, but we ought to have the benefit of your suggestions as to how this change ought to be brought about.

MR. CARPENTER: I move the adoption of the amendment.

MR. CHARLES G. DAWES: I second the motion.

MR. GLESSNER: May I say a word? With this large vacancy as it has been made, it will be impossible to fill it by one name at a meeting. We have had some bitter experiences with reference to not offering more than one. I think that ought to be very carefully considered. I do not know as I quite understood what you said a while ago. If there are two or more candidates at one time, there will be a separate ballot for each candidate, is that correct?

PRESIDENT SUNNY: Yes, and we have tried to specify the type of members that we want; that is, "citizens eligible for membership by reason of their personality, general reputation, and their contributions in effective interest and service to the common welfare."

MR. GLESSNER: The point I wish to bring out is this: I don't want to go into details, but there were three members in line, every one of whom was eligible. The result of it finally was that they were elected, but it took quite some time. I think in view of the possible dangers there might be in it, that they ought to be very carefully considered before they are elected.

PRESIDENT SUNNY: The last sentence reads, "If the names of two or more nominees are printed on the ballot, opportunity will be given to cast a separate vote for each nominee."

MR. BUFFINGTON: I think that covers it. Mr. President, does that mean that more than one nominee can be voted upon at a meeting?

PRESIDENT SUNNY: Yes, sir.

MR. BUFFINGTON: That is what I understand. That covers it, Mr. Glessner.

PRESIDENT SUNNY: You can elect ten at a meeting. Are you ready for the question?

(The question was called for, and on a viva voce vote the motion was unanimously carried.)

PRESIDENT SUNNY: The next is the amendment to Section 8, Article I, "In the approval of candidates regard shall be had, so far as practicable, to the branches of business or professions in which they are engaged, so that the various interests of the city shall be fairly represented in the membership."

MR. ELTING: I move its adoption.

MR. CHARLES G. DAWES: I second the motion.

(On a viva voce vote the motion was unanimously carried.)

PRESIDENT SUNNY: The next amendment is with reference to the number of members on the Executive Committee, a change from ten to twelve, to take care of the increase in membership.

MR. ROSENWALD: I move it be adopted.

MR. BUFFINGTON: I second the motion.

(On a viva voce vote the motion was unanimously carried.)

PRESIDENT SUNNY: The last amendment to be considered is the one which proposed to do away with the February and March meetings of the Club; to begin our meetings in October, that is, meetings will be held in October, November, December, January—skip February and March—and have meetings in April and May. The attendance in those two months, February and March, according to the statistics, is such that there are twenty to twenty-five fewer men here in February and March than at other times. It not only means a very slim attendance at the Club meetings, but it also means a very large percentage of our Club members are deprived of being at the meetings because they cannot be here. I have talked with a great many members and this seems to fit in with the present situation.

MR. ROSENWALD: I move the adoption of the amendment.

MR. CHARLES G. DAWES: I second the motion.

MR. FORGAN: Just as a matter of information, Mr. President, would that mean that the annual meeting would be held in April or May?

PRESIDENT SUNNY: In May. I will put the motion.

(On a viva voce vote the motion was unanimously carried.)

PRESIDENT SUNNY: The next business is the report of the Nominating Committee, Mr. David R. Forgan, Chairman.

MR. DAVID R. FORGAN; Mr. President, the following is the report of the Nominating Committee for officers of the Club for the ensuing year:

For President: Mr. Harry A. Wheeler.

For Vice-President: Mr. Frederic W. Upham.

For Secretary: Mr. George E. Scott.

For Treasurer: Mr. Albert W. Harris.

For Members of the Executive Committee, to serve two years: Mr. Robert W. Stewart, Mr. Clarence S. Pellett.

For Reception Committee: Mr. Wallace C. Winter, Chairman; Mr. William P. Sidley, Mr. John Stuart, Mr. Leonard A. Busby, Mr. Robert J. Thorne.

I move you, Mr. Chairman, that the Secretary cast the unanimous ballot for the election of these gentlemen.

(There were many seconds to the motion, and on a viva voce vote the motion was unanimously carried.)

PRESIDENT SUNNY: I am very sorry that Mr. Wheeler could not be with us tonight. He is on his way to the Pacific Coast to raise money for the United States Chamber of Commerce. I am sorry also that our Vice-President, Mr. Frederic W. Upham, cannot be with us tonight.

I have a telegram from Mr. Upham, from Washington, which I received yesterday, which says:

"The President will surely accept the invitation of the Commercial Club for dinner when in Chicago. Frederic W. Upham."

Gentlemen, this concludes our program and I want to thank you very sincerely for coming here this evening.

MR. SPRAGUE: Mr. President, I would like to move that the Club go on record expressing its gratitude to Mr. Sunny for the entertainment this evening.

(There were many seconds to the motion and a rising vote of thanks was given Mr. Sunny, after which the meeting adjourned.)

Necrology

Club Year 1922-1923

The Commercial Club of Chicago

THE COMMERCIAL CLUB, ORGANIZED 1877
THE MERCHANTS CLUB, ORGANIZED 1896
UNITED 1907

ADOLPHUS CLAY BARTLETT

ADOLPHUS CLAY BARTLETT

Resolutions Adopted at the Two Hundred and Eighty-second Regular Meeting, November 17, 1923.

The Members of the Commercial Club record with sorrow the death of one of the oldest and most highly esteemed members of the Club—Adolphus Clay Bartlett—who died at Pasadena, California, on the thirtieth day of May, Nineteen Hundred and Twenty-two. Born in New York State on the twenty-second day of June, Eighteen Hundred and Forty-four, he came to Chicago at the early age of nineteen and became one of the most successful merchants of this city. He was a fine example of the successful business man. In addition he was a public-spirited citizen who gave much time and service to the community in which he lived. For many years he has given freely of his money, time and energy to the upbuilding of the educational and charitable institutions of Chicago. He served for a short time on the Board of Education of this city; was Trustee of the University of Chicago, the Art Institute of Chicago, Central Church and Beloit College. For many years he served as President of the Chicago Home for the Friendless. For forty years he was a Member of the Commercial Club. In recognition of his standing in the business and philanthropic work of Chicago, he was elected its President in Eighteen Hundred and Eighty-six. He possessed in a high degree those qualities which we have always insisted upon as prerequisite for membership in our organization.

By means of these Resolutions we wish not only to give

expression to our sorrow, but to extend our heartfelt sympathy to the members of Mr. Bartlett's family.

MARVIN HUGHITT, *Chairman,*
C. L. HUTCHINSON,
Committee.

RENSSELAER W. COX

RENSSELAER W. COX

Resolutions Adopted at the Two Hundred and Eighty-second Regular Meeting, November 17, 1923

The members of The Commercial Club are called upon to record the death of one of its highly esteemed members—Rensselaer W. Cox, who died in Chicago on the twenty-sixth day of September, Nineteen Hundred Twenty-two. He joined the Merchants Club in 1899, becoming a member of The Commercial Club by the union of the two Clubs in 1907. Mr. Cox displayed marked ability in the conduct of his business, achieving the foremost position among his competitors, all of whom were his friends. Not only was he a man of marked ability and forceful character, but one who endeared himself to all his friends by his modesty and courteous manner. He was never aggressive, but always a man of fixed and firm convictions. Owing to failing health he retired from Active Membership in the Club in 1910, and since that time has been among its Associate Members.

With deep regret the members of the Club record his death, and express their appreciation of his friendship and genial companionship.

ERNEST A. HAMILL, *Chairman,*
SAMUEL INSULL,
C. L. HUTCHINSON,
Committee.

CHARLES DYER NORTON

CHARLES DYER NORTON

Resolutions Adopted at the Two Hundred and Eighty-seventh Regular Meeting, April 13, 1923

Among the illustrious names that death has taken from the membership roll of the Commercial Club, there is no other that represents so much of accomplishment, in so short a lifetime, as that of Charles Dyer Norton, our beloved fellow member, who died on March sixth, Nineteen Hundred and Twenty-three.

He was born in Oshkosh, Wisconsin, March 12, 1871, and graduated from Amherst in 1893, after which he went into the services of *Scribner's Magazine*. Subsequently he was with the Northwestern Mutual Life Insurance Company in Chicago from 1895 to 1909, when be became Assistant Secretary of the Treasury of the United States, which office he filled for one year when he was appointed Secretary to President Taft. In 1911 he retired from the Government service to become Vice-president of the First National Bank of New York.

He was a director in many important banks and corporations. He was a Trustee in the American Red Cross, Metropolitan Museum of Art, American Academy in Rome, American Federation of Arts, Russell Sage Foundation.

These various positions of great trust in themselves tell the story of his extraordinary industry and activity.

In that comparatively short period of his business career in Chicago, we knew him mostly as one of the organizers of the Merchants Club, its Secretary in 1904-06 and its President in 1906-07, and an earnest and extremely helpful Member of the Commercial Club, of which he was Chairman of the Committee on Plan of Chicago up to the time he became a Non-resident Member.

Charles Norton was a man of such impelling personality, he had such a genius for making and holding friends, that we all loved him and his death is a real personal bereavement.

He was remarkable in many ways. He was a man of vision. He was not only a dreamer of beautiful dreams, but he was a constructive builder. He was an ideal citizen, ever ready to give of himself unsparingly. He was an altruist who reached out into the larger fields of usefulness.

His enthusiasm was so contagious that he was able to draw about him conservative men of mature years and fire them with his ardor.

It was Charles Dyer Norton who, with his friend and collaborator, Frederick Delano, induced Daniel H. Burnham to take up the great work of making a plan of Chicago.

That same enthusiasm, that same devotion to public duty, without regard for health or personal interests, he carried with him to New York. There, too, he has set on foot the creation of a great plan for New York and its environs. This plan is being made and when it is completed it will, for all time, be a monument to the devotion of Charles Dyer Norton to the cause of civic betterment, to the idea of better cities, better homes and better men and women.

In appreciation of the life and work of our beloved friend, of his loyal friendship, his patriotic citizenship, and his many and remarkable achievements, we write this minute into the records of the Commercial Club, and we express to Mrs. Norton and her family the assurances of our profound and sincere sympathy, in their severe bereavement.

EDWARD B. BUTLER,
CHARLES H. WACKER,
DONALD R. MCLENNAN,
Committee.

EDMUND DANIEL HULBERT

EDMUND DANIEL HULBERT

Resolutions Adopted at the Two Hundred Eighty-seventh Regular Meeting, April 13, 1923

Edmund Daniel Hulbert, for many years a member of the Commercial Club of Chicago, passed away at his home, 191 East Walton Place, Chicago, on March 30, 1923. He was a man of rugged and forceful character—courageous in times of stress, direct and straightforward in word and deed—of unswerving integrity, of undeviating loyalty and tireless and persevering industry.

Intensely human, he was always considerate and kindly; his fairness of thought and his lively sense of humor endeared him to all with whom he came in contact.

In the financial affairs of the nation he was a potent factor. While for personal reasons he declined to accept high office, yet he was the trusted advisor of the nation's president, and perhaps more than any other man shaped and helped to successfully launch our present monetary system.

He was deeply interested in boys, and in founding the Boys Brotherhood Republic, a "government of boys, by boys and for boys," he adopted the basic principle of his conception of an executive, which was that "responsibility develops character."

His death came at the zenith of his career—just as he was about to accomplish his greatest business achievement, the physical consolidation of the three great banks of which he was president.

He leaves to mourn his loss a host of friends and his devoted wife, to whom we extend our deepest sympathy. The world is better for his having lived.

JOHN J. MITCHELL, *Chairman*,
B. A. ECKHART,
CHAUNCEY KEEP,
Committee.

Lightning Source UK Ltd.
Milton Keynes UK
UKHW012144140219
337323UK00012B/799/P